CW01639074

It's a very special day

Helping families celebrate Christian festivals

Donated to St. Bartholomew's Church by the Christian Bookshop, Gt. Clacton.

Written by Christine Elliott Hall, Judy Jarvis and Mary Jefferson

Illustrated by Wendy Carolan and Phillip Vernon

Cover design by Image-On Artworks

Edited by Elizabeth Bruce

Published by:
National Christian Education Council
1020 Bristol Road
Selly Oak
Birmingham
B29 6LB

British Cataloguing-in-Publication Data:
A catalogue record for this book is available from the British Library.

ISBN 0-7197-0943-1

First published 1998

Designed and typeset by National Christian Education Council.
Printed and bound by Halcyon, East Sussex

Contents

It's a very special day is about marking the Christian year – all of it, not just Christmas Day. It is about the family at home, celebrating every part of life.

Where do we start?

All celebrations and festivals need:

❋ Story

For Christians the starting point is the Bible story. Alongside are other stories which help our understanding: stories of real people in real situations, stories from imagination and, of great importance, stories from our own experience. All these stories come together to help us in our understanding of The Story.

❋ Symbol

Symbols give us pictures when words are not enough. They help to 'access the mystery'. Symbols are often familiar, everyday objects and materials which act as springboards for a deeper understanding of those things which are not easily spoken about.

❋ Togetherness

By its very nature, celebration is a shared experience. The family group is an obvious place for this to happen. It is the place where there are good times, bad times, fun and friction, delight and anxiety – the whole range of human life.

❋ Reflection and action

As human beings, we feel the need to make sense of our lives and to affirm each other. For example, in families and with friends, we mark birthdays as one way of showing how each person is loved and valued. As Christians we recognize that God shares with us in all the experiences of life.

All this comes together to shape our own family traditions and celebrations so that, quite quickly, families can say, 'We always...'. At the same time, it is important to recognize that some celebrations need to stay the same, whilst others will change as we grow and develop.

Families celebrating

Christian festivals provide a wonderful opportunity for family celebration. They are a time for playing and dreaming with God and discovering God in all of life. Often a festival looks like a party, celebrating something good such as the birth of Jesus at Christmas. Some festivals, Good Friday for example, are much more sober. All are important.

Many Christian festivals have their roots in ancient traditions and rituals linked to the seasons of the year. Christmas is based on the winter solstice, the mid-winter festival of light. Now we celebrate Jesus, the light of the world, coming into the darkness.

Easter's date is set by the spring moon and derives from a festival linked with rebirth, fertility and spring. The ancient symbols of hare and egg, both known as signs of the return of life after winter's sleep, today carry the Christian association of the resurrection of Christ. When we exchange Easter eggs we are re-enacting an ancient wisdom – that which appears to be still and dead in fact contains new life. Nature and mystery are combined.

The cycle of festivals in the Church year, beginning with Advent, comes from events in the life of Jesus and what God has done for us through him. Meaning and shape are given to our lives and a sense of order is given to time. As we celebrate festivals we recognize that we are living in God's time. That is why every Sunday, the day of Jesus' being raised from death, is also a festival, a time for celebration.

Festivals and stories are inextricably linked. As we hear the stories and pick up traditions and memories, we find that we are part of an ongoing story and we remember where we have come from. Symbol, myth, ritual and ceremony both link us to our forebears, to our ancient roots, and take us forward into the future through our children.

In celebrations and rituals we often use symbols which are ordinary elements of everyday life. Through what is familiar they give us glimpses of God. So bread, wine, fire, ash, earth, water, oil, tears, feasting and fasting, all have a part to play. We are used to thinking of them in a church context. Do we ever think of using them at home? Taking 'time out' at home to celebrate holy days brings together the ordinary and the extraordinary. We are refreshed and our spirits are fed. We look backwards and forwards and recognize God in our common experience.

In all of this, colours are important. Many churches use them in different ways to mark the seasons of the Church year, as is shown in the song 'The Rainbow Year' (see page 8).

Many of the ceremonies and rituals involve making things together, which can be an important feature of family life. Obvious examples are music-making, drama and painting. Doing these sorts of things together can be very important in family life and integral to the celebration. Another good example is the preparation, serving and eating of food. Celebrations are great opportunities for hospitality as well as for building up the family in faith. Sharing with others can bring new insights and opportunities.

Every member of a family needs to be fully involved in celebrating, each in their own way. Where a leader is required, this does not always have to be an adult. Being aware of the meaning, theme and focus of the celebration is more important than age.

'Celebration is the spontaneous expression of joy, created through memory. The core of Christian faith is that kind of celebration created by the historic Jesus, but Jesus is not locked in the past; he is present with us, and he invites us from the future to follow him. So Christian celebration brings together past, present and future.'

(Chris Hughes Smith)

The Rainbow Year

When Noah's ark was high and dry,
there came a rainbow in the sky
and Noah heard a voice divine:
'I am your God and you are mine.'

This God, who ever faithful stays,
has given colour to our days.
The shade with which the year begins
is purple for the people's sins.

On Christmas-day we see the light,
– the colour of the feast is white –
and when the Kings have left the scene,
our life runs into days of green.

With purple we return in Lent,
to mourn for Jesus,emptied,spent.
But sorrow is not meant to stay,
proclaims the white of Easter-day!

As red as flames of Pentecost,
so is the blood the martyrs lost.
Then, till the hopeful Advent sound,
we make with green the circle round.

The people of the church are led
through purple, white and green and red,
from fasting times to peaks of feast
from dark of death to life in Christ!

(by Fred Kaan)

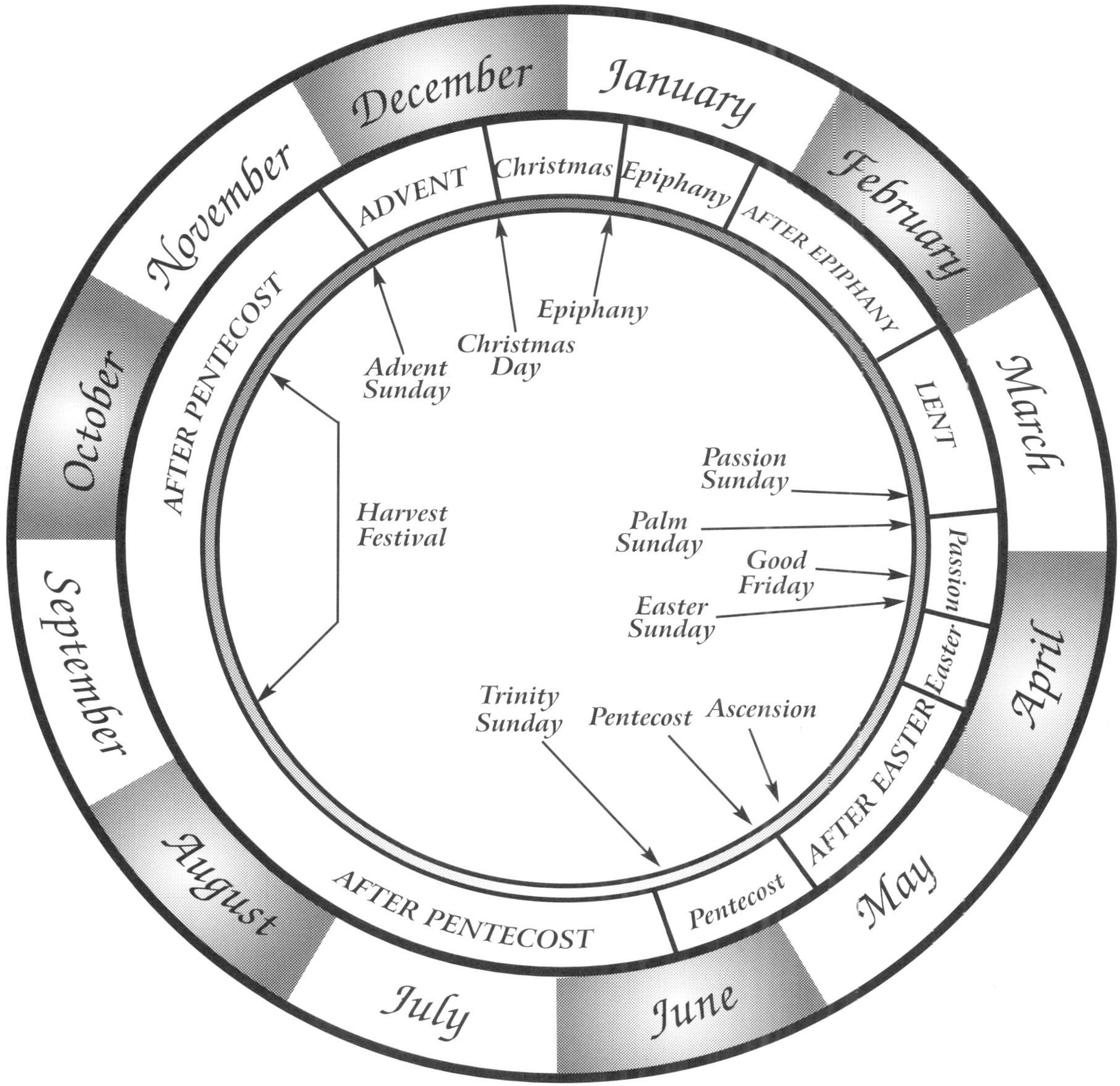

January
February
March
April
May
June
July
August
September
October
November
December
ADVENT
Christmas
Epiphany
AFTER EPIPHANY
LENT
Passion
Easter
AFTER EASTER
Pentecost
AFTER PENTECOST
AFTER PENTECOST
Advent Sunday
Christmas Day
Epiphany
Passion Sunday
Palm Sunday
Good Friday
Easter Sunday
Ascension
Pentecost
Trinity Sunday
Harvest Festival

GOD COMING TO US

Colours – purple and white or gold

What are we celebrating?

Advent is a time of looking forward, particularly to the coming of Jesus.

A time for:

- preparing ourselves for Jesus' coming;
- expectation and hope;
- watching and waiting;
- awe and wonder;
- welcoming the Christ.

During the period of Advent, we are not only preparing to celebrate Jesus' birth but also anticipating his return. In Advent we get ready for Christmas. The church uses purple to remind us of this preparation, as it does in Lent when we prepare for Easter. We are prepared for the momentous event of the Incarnation by reading again the Old Testament stories of the prophets and patriarchs and the Gospel accounts of John the Baptist.

At **Christmas** we celebrate Christ's birth – Joy to the World.

Epiphany is about the showing of Jesus to the wise men; the festival celebrates the 'showing forth' of Jesus to the whole world.

What are the traditions?

❊ The Church's **traditional colours** are: *purple* for **Advent** and *white* or *gold* for **Christmas** to **Epiphany**.

Candles and **lights**, echoing the Star, symbolize joy and happiness, light in the darkness.

Christingles symbolize Jesus, the Light of the World.

❊ **Advent:**

- setting up a Christmas crib;
- preparing special foods;
- building up expectation through Advent rings and Advent calendars;
- carol-singing.

❊ **Christmas**:

- eating special foods;
- exchanging presents; gifts brought by Saint Nicholas;
- decorating Christmas trees and bringing evergreens into the house;
- going to church;
- families being together.

- **Epiphany**:
  - the coming of the wise men is celebrated. In some countries, this is the main celebration of Christmas and the time when gifts are exchanged.
  - the twelfth day of Christmas;
  - taking down decorations.

What stories lead us in?

- Isaiah 9.2-7
  (The people who walked in darkness)
- Luke 1.76-80
  (Zechariah's prophecy about John the Baptist)
- Luke 1.26-38
  (The Annunciation)
- Luke 1.39-56
  (Mary's visit to Elizabeth and the *Magnificat*)
- Matthew 1.18-24
  (Joseph's dream about the birth of Jesus)

What can we do to prepare?

- Make an **Advent wreath** for the table. Make a ring-shape using either wire, a posy ring filled with sand, a thick cake board or florist's 'oasis'. Decorate it with evergreens. Stick four purple or red candles into the base, as illustrated (potatoes make good holders). Place a taller white candle in the centre.
- Make a simple evergreen **Advent wreath** and hang it on the front door to tell everyone that you think the season is special.
- Use an **Advent calendar**. Find or make one in which the windows open onto pictures or symbols to do with the coming of Jesus or, as in Christian Aid ones, show how people in other parts of the world get ready for Christmas. If you make one you may find it easier to have only four windows, one for each Sunday.
- Make an **Advent paper chain of prayer**. Add a new link every day. On each link, write a hope or prayer for yourself, your family, a particular person or the world.

Prayer and Reflection

The world was in darkness
And nobody knew
The way to the Father
As you and I do.
They needed a light
That would show them the way;
And the great light shone
On Christmas Day.
(Sr. Mary Oswin)

I saw a stable, low and very bare,
A little child in a manger,
The oxen knew him, had him in their care.
To men he was a stranger.
The safety of the world was lying there
And the world's danger.
(Mary Coleridge)

Advent – preparing the way

What are we celebrating?

Advent has traditionally been a season for penitence. It is also a time of expectation and hope when we wait for God's coming and begin to understand that God judges us in love.

Where are the stories?

Bible stories

- Isaiah 52.1-10
  (God sends a messenger)
- Mark 1.1-6
  (John the Baptist prepares the way)
- 2 Peter 1.19
  (Listen to the prophets' message)

Other stories

- *Papa Panov's Special Day*
  Retold by Mig Holder (Lion)
- *Burglar Bill*
  Janet Ahlberg and Allan Ahlberg (Puffin)
- *The Snow Queen*
  Hans Christian Andersen (Puffin)
- *The Little Match Girl*
  Hans Christian Andersen

What can we do to celebrate?

Make

A Jesse tree

'A shoot will come up from the stump of Jesse' (Isaiah 11.1, NIV). Use a bare branch, twigs or a sturdy potted plant. Hang symbols on it to represent stories as they are told during Advent. Start with characters from the Old Testament such as Adam (apple), Noah (ark), Joseph (coat of many colours) and David (crown).

A prophet lantern

You will need: paper; scissors; felt-tipped pens or crayons; a clean jam jar; glue; a nightlight; blu-tak or double-sided tape.

Make a chain of paper dolls, as shown in the diagrams above. Using the felt-tipped pens or crayons, colour in and decorate the figures to represent prophets – either prophets from the Old Testament, or modern people whom you regard as prophets in some way.

Glue the chain of figures around the outside of the jam jar. Put the nightlight inside the jar, using the blu-tak or double-sided tape to keep it in place.

Before you light the candle, think of someone you know who challenges people about how they treat others and live in the world. Think of someone who is a 'star' – a shining example, fiery, bright, brilliant, and sunny.

Advent leaves

Cut leaf shapes out of paper, large enough to write on.

Turning over a new leaf for myself

On one side of your leaf, draw a sad face and write something that you are sorry for doing. On the other side, draw a smiling face and write down how you will change your behaviour in the week to come. Talk about God's forgiveness when we say sorry.

Turning over a new leaf for the world

On one side of your leaf, draw a sad face and write something that you see in the world that makes you feel sad or sorry (e.g. people fighting each other, people going hungry, or rich countries not trading fairly with poor countries). On the other side, draw a smiling face and write down how you would like to see justice in this situation and what you might do (e.g. use fairly-traded goods or save money to send to an appropriate charity).

Eat

Sunday lunch

Make Sunday lunch special, putting the Advent wreath on the table. Invite a guest to eat with you. You might like to have a child ask questions similar to those asked at the Jewish Passover, using the following script:

Child: What are we celebrating today?
Adult: We are celebrating the Advent of Jesus Christ our Lord.

Child: What is Advent? What does it mean?
Adult: In Advent we remember especially that Jesus Christ came on earth when our ancestors in Israel had been prepared for him, and we look forward to his promised return again in glory.
Child: What does the first candle stand for?
Adult: For us, watching and waiting.
Child: What does the second candle stand for?
Adult: The prophets, shining in the darkness.
Child: What does the third candle stand for?
Adult: John the Baptist, preparing the way.
Child: What does the fourth candle stand for?
Adult: Mother Mary, obeying God.

Sing

'One red candle shining bright' (*Hymns and Songs*)

'The holly and the ivy are dancing in a ring' (*Hymns and Psalms*)

'Christmas is coming' (*Innkeepers and Light Sleepers*. Wild Goose)

'It's hard to say I'm sorry' (*Big Blue Planet*)

Listen

Extracts from *Messiah* (Handel)

Carols, old and new

Prepare ye the way (Godspell)

Look

Sit in the darkness for a few minutes, then light a candle.

Go outside and gaze at the stars and moon on a clear night.

Make an evening trip into town to admire the Christmas decorations.

What does it all add up to?

Questions

What is the difference between being selfish and loving myself as in 'love your neighbour as yourself'?

Why does a loving God judge?

How does a loving God forgive? How do we forgive?

Insight

God prepares people but we have to work at it. It's worth waiting!

Actions

Turn over a new leaf!

Pray for those who are going through hard times. Do something to help.

Invite someone (e.g. an overseas student) to share a meal.

Prayer and Reflection

When the world began
God said yes
When Jesus came
God said yes
When we were born
God said yes
God says yes to life and loving
God calls us
To be like Mary
God calls us
To life and loving.
God, when you call us, help us to say yes.
(Author unknown)

God, you took a long time to get ready for Jesus
I've only got four weeks, please help me.
(Anon)

What are we celebrating?

Christmas is coming and preparations of all kinds need to be made, both practical and spiritual.

Where are the stories?

Bible stories

- Luke 1.26-38
  (The Annunciation)
- Luke 2.1-5
  (Mary and Joseph go to Bethlehem)

Other stories

- *The Christmas Story*
  Dick Bruna (Methuen)
- *Lights* (Teddy Horsley series)
  Leslie J Francis and Nicola M Slee (NCEC)
- *Haffertee's First Christmas*
  Janet and John Perkins (Lion)
- *The Fox's Tale*
  Butterworth and Inkpen (Collins/Lions)
- *Christmas in Exeter Street*
  Diana Hendry (Walker Books)
- *The Wind in the Willows*
  Kenneth Grahame (Methuen)
- *The Lion, the Witch and the Wardrobe*
  CS Lewis (Collins/Lions) or BBC Video
- *The Country Child*
  Alison Uttley (Collins)
- *The Elves and the Shoemaker*
  Brothers Grimm
- *Can it be true?*
  Susan Hill (Walker Books)

What can we do to celebrate?

Cook

Christmas cake

Let children help to ice it, perhaps with a snow scene.

Mince pies

These were traditionally oval, like a crib. Put a small pastry star on top instead of a lid.

Food from another country

Sample food such as German *stollen* (a kind of cake with fruit in it) or Danish cookies.

Eat

A frugal meal

Put money saved into a 'jar of grace' and send to Christian Aid or another charity.

Go

Why not go carolling as a family? Collect money for NCH Action for Children, Barnardo's or another children's charity. Remember to use an official collecting tin.

Do

Put together a nativity play, drafting in friends and relatives to take the various roles. Alternatively, use the figures you made for the stable scene. Invite friends and neighbours to the performance.

Make

A piñata

In Mexico, children are given small gifts in a *piñata*, a brightly-coloured clay pot, traditionally in the shape of a bull. This is hung up before Christmas, and then knocked down by the children on Christmas Day.

You will need: card; brown paper (tissue breaks satisfactorily when you bash it, but wrapping paper is stronger); a cane; staples or glue; string; sweets; crepe paper.

Cut a bull's head, tail and legs from the card, and cut two rough 'body' shapes from the brown paper. Cut and glue crepe paper fringes on one side of each body shape. Place the sweets on the undecorated side of one of the body shapes, and staple the head, tail and legs in position on the same body shape. Place the cane along the top edge of that body shape, and staple or glue the second body piece in position:

Attach string to either end of the cane, and hang up the piñata. Bash the paper body thoroughly to release the sweets!

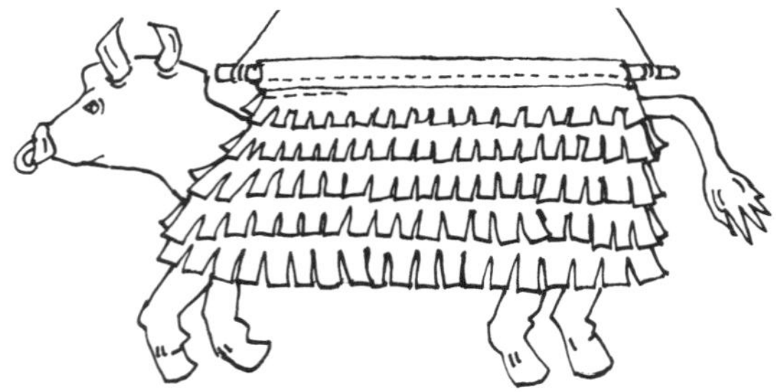

Chrismons for the Christmas tree

You will need: white card or thin polystyrene; scissors or a sharp knife; gold glitter glue, gold paint, etc.; thread or wool.
Cut the card or polystyrene into the shapes of Christian symbols associated with Christmas, e.g. angel, candle, dove, lamb, star, trumpet and bell.

Decorate with the glitter glue and/or paint. Chrismons are traditionally white or gold. Use the thread to hang them from the Christmas tree.

A stable scene

Use cardboard cylinders to make the nativity figures. Pinch the top to form the head. Make slits for arms about one third of the way down. Decorate with paper, wool and fabric. Keep the crib empty until Christmas Day.

Christmas cards, gift wrap, tags

Make your own design, with potato prints of stars, holly leaves and/or candles.

Gifts

Make sweets, mince pies, biscuits, calendars, etc. Find imaginative ways of wrapping them.

Sing

'Come, Lord Jesus, come' (*Big Blue Planet*)

'Who came to Mary?' (*Big Blue Planet*)

'Standing in the rain' (*Sing Round the Year*)

Listen

Saint Nicholas by Benjamin Britten

Have you heard any carol singers yet?

What does it all add up to?

? Questions

How can God, who is great, become one of us?

How do we recognize God's coming to us?

☆ Insights

Making and doing things for ourselves and others takes us away from the routine and opens our hearts to receive the Christ-child.

➔ Actions

In the midst of the rush and bustle of Christmas, make time for each other.

Share in a local Christmas project.

Prayer and Reflection

At Advent we should try the key to our heart's door.
It may have gathered rust.
If so, this is the time to oil it,
in order that the heart's door may open more easily
when the Lord Jesus wants to enter
at Christmas time.
(A Christian from New Guinea)

Christmas

What are we celebrating?

Jesus came, and comes, to be one of us. Traditionally people have celebrated the turn of the winter solstice, the lengthening of the days, the coming again of the sun. Now we celebrate the coming of the Son, God with us.

Where are the stories?

Bible stories

- Luke 2.1-7
  (The birth of Jesus in Bethlehem)
- Luke 2.8-18
  (The angels and the shepherds)

Other stories

- *Christmas*
  Jan Pienkowski (Heinemann)
- *The Singing Shepherd*
  Angela Elwell Hunt (Lion)
- *A Christmas Carol*
  Charles Dickens
- *The gift* (Short story)
  O Henry

What can we do to celebrate?

On Christmas Eve

Stable scene

Set up the crib (but leave the figure of the Christ child until tomorrow).

Candle in the window

Follow the tradition of putting a candle in the window on Christmas Eve to guide Mary and Joseph to shelter.

Christingle

Make a Christingle (Christ light).

You will need: an orange; a candle; four cocktail sticks; nuts and fruits; a red ribbon; tin foil.

Tie the ribbon round the orange. Cut a round hole in the top of the orange to hold the candle. Wrap the tin foil round the base of the candle, then place the candle in the hole in the orange. Spread out the tin foil and trim it to make a star shape.

Thread the fruits and nuts onto the cocktail sticks. Stick the cocktail sticks into the orange, around the candle.

Christmas stockings

Hang up stockings for everyone.

Nine lessons and carols

Listen to or watch a service of nine lessons and carols, if you are unable to attend one.

Last-minute preparations

Encourage everyone to help prepare the special food.

Advent calendar

Open the last window on your Advent calendar.

On Christmas Day

Stable scene

Put the figure of the Christ child in the crib. Place the figures of the Wise Men (Magi) in the room, but not close to the crib. After today, move them closer each day until Epiphany.

Advent wreath

Light the white candle. Add some coloured baubles. Light the four outer candles.

Christingle

At the special meal put the Christingle in the centre of the table. Light it and think about the symbolism: the orange for the world; the candle for the Light of the World; the red ribbon for the blood of Christ, shed for the world; the cocktail sticks for the four seasons; the fruits and nuts for the fruits of the earth.

Mince pies

When you eat a mince pie, think of Jesus being born in a manger in a stable 'because there was no room at the inn'. Pray for people who are sad this Christmas.

Presents

Make a special time for sharing presents (even if some have been opened very early in the day). Enjoy each other's pleasure as gifts are unwrapped.

Music and singing

Sing 'Yea, Lord, we greet thee, born this happy morning' from 'O come, all ye faithful'.

Make music together: sing some carols; play all the instruments you have, or improvise!

Sharing the day

Invite a guest (perhaps someone who would otherwise be on their own) to share some of the day – make it clear how much!

Fresh air

Go for a walk. Stop and be quiet for a few minutes. What can you see? What can you hear?

Games

Play some games together.

What does it all add up to?

Question

Can we make every day in some sense a Christmas Day?

Insights

The gifts we share are not just the presents we buy, but the way we live our lives.

When we love other people we love Jesus and when others love us they do the same.

Action

'Dear friends, let us love one another, because love comes from God.' (1 John 4.7)

Prayer and Reflection

Not for him a big white ambulance
But a slow donkey.
Not for him flashing blue lights
But the Star of Bethlehem.
Not for him the white hospital wards
But a cold stable.
Not for him a nice warm cradle
But a manger full of straw.
Not for him fleecy babygrows
But plain swaddling bands.
Not for him the midwife, nurse and doctors
But three simple shepherds.
Not for him auntie and uncle from the north
But Three Kings from the east.
Not for him a cuddly teddy bear
But a shepherd boy's lamb.
Not for him a silver coin in his palm
But frankincense, myrrh and gold.
Not for him a future in computers
But the Crown of Heaven.

(Daniel Salsedo, age 11)

What are we celebrating?

Epiphany, which means 'showing forth', marks the arrival of 'the wise men' (Magi), who followed a star which excited them. It led them to the child Jesus, in whom they recognized something very special.

Where are the stories?

Bible stories

- Matthew 2.1-12
  (The visit of the Magi led by a star)
- Luke 2.25-35
  (Simeon recognizes Jesus as being for all people)

Other stories

- *Presents* (Teddy Horsley series)
  Leslie J Francis and Nicola M Slee (NCEC)
- *Baboushka*
  Retold by Arthur Whaley (Lion)
- *Caspar and the Star*
  Francesca Bosca (Lion)
- 'A Single Star', in *The Mayor and the Simpleton*
  Ian Serraillier (Puffin)
- *The Story of the other Wise Man*
  Henry Van Dyke (Hodder and Stoughton)
- *The Epiphany Tree*
  (See page 24)

What can we do to celebrate?

Move on

Take down the Christmas decorations, but leave the stable scene in place. Move the Magi into a prominent position

If you have read the story of *Baboushka* you may like to add a Russian doll to the stable scene.

Make

Stars

Use gold-coloured card or paper, glitter etc. to make stars in gold, the liturgical colour. Make many different ones and turn them into a collage or mobile.

Epiphany cards

Stick stars or crowns onto card to make an Epiphany card. Inside write some appropriate words such as: 'Jesus is King, worship and serve him'. Send it to someone who is special to you or who might be feeling lonely.

Crowns

Make paper crowns to remind you that Jesus is the king for whom the Wise Men were searching, and also our king.

Stained glass

Make an Epiphany 'stained glass window' or mobile.

You will need: sheets of greaseproof paper; felt-tipped pens; black card; a ruler; scissors or a sharp knife; glue.

Use a thick black felt-tipped pen to draw your design on greaseproof paper. Remember to leave space round the edges for the frame. Colour in the shapes.

Make a frame for your window using the black card. Glue the greaseproof paper onto the back of the frame.

Stick it to a window with blu-tak.

This idea can be adapted to make shapes to hang from a mobile.

Listen

Amahl and the Night Visitors. Menotti

Do

Have an Epiphany party with a Twelfth Night cake, such as the French 'Galette des Rois'. Use a basic madeira cake recipe and add grated lemon rind, one dried bean, one dried pea, and, if you wish, some trinkets. Decorate it with stars, crowns or three kings. The person who finds the bean is king; the one who finds the pea is queen for the party. They wear crowns and lead the games.

Read on

In Matthew 2.12-21, read how Herod killed baby boys in order to get rid of Jesus (another king to challenge him?) and how Jesus and his family became refugees. Pray for refugees today. Think of how joy and sadness get mixed up, especially where power is involved.

What does it all add up to?

? **Questions**

Why did the Magi come into the story?

How could God risk the possibility of the baby Jesus being murdered?

☆ **Insights**

God breaks into our lives – often in unexpected ways.

A baby is vulnerable and needs love to survive. In Jesus, God shows us how love makes us vulnerable but also gives us strength.

➜ **Actions**

Pray that those who have power may exercise it wisely (even parents in the family and teachers in school!).

Make a special gift for a baby you know and take it to him or her. Explain to the baby's family what prompted you to do this.

Be vulnerable! Don't pretend to know all the answers.

Prayer and Reflection

It looks much as it did before,
Now that the cards and decorations
Have come down.
The furniture of life is back in place,
The old routine takes over.
But are we the same?
Is there no echo of the angel's song
Lifting our spirits, no stillness
In our hearts, reminding us that
We were there, just for a moment
At that birth,
Catching a glimpse of glory?
Let's not put that away,
Tangled with tinsel, for another time.
Let's ponder in our hearts, like Mary,
And let the child grow with us
Through the year.
(Ann Lewin)

...Were we led all that way for
Birth and Death? There was a Birth, certainly,
We had evidence and no doubt. I had seen birth and death,
But had thought they were different: this Birth was
Hard and bitter agony for us, like Death, our death.
(T.S. Eliot: 'Journey of the Magi')

They all were looking for a king
To slay their foes, and lift them high;
Thou cam'st, a little baby thing,
That made a woman cry.
(George MacDonald)

The story of the Epiphany Tree

Once there was a little fir tree. It stood in amongst other fir trees which were much bigger. It was a beautiful place with grass and flowers growing all around. Creatures lived and moved there. The fir tree liked the surroundings a great deal but best of all she liked to look up at the sky. The sky could be clear and crystal blue, or full of clouds moving swiftly or slowly; it could be grey and full of rain, or it could be dark and full of stars. It was when it was starry and glittering that the little fir tree liked it best of all. In fact she wished it was possible to get up into the sky.

One winter night something quite remarkable happened. A bright light shone and the tree was being moved. Could it be that she was going to heaven? Maybe it was possible to get up to the sky after all. After a short journey the tree was taken to a house. Inside it was warm and then strange things happened. Decorations such as stars and flowers, lights and gold ribbon, and even fruit were being draped over her branches. Perhaps these decorations were part of the preparation for going to heaven. But then something else happened: a door opened and in rushed some children. They gasped and then shouted with glee and excitement and it was all so thrilling that the tree forgot all about heaven. It was now time to give as much as she could for the children.

So for the twelve days of Christmas the fir tree stood tall and proud, giving off her wonderful scent. On the twelfth day the children came bouncing into the room and this time started stripping the tree of all the decorations – some of them had already gone because they had been eaten! The tree was taken outside again where she was pushed into a dark hole. Oh, it was so sad. A flame licked up to the tree's needles and branches and it was so hot. A searing pain of fire gripped her yet it was glowing, a different kind of glowing this time. The branches gleamed from within; they were bright and golden and warm. The fir tree lit up and found the wood was left behind and she became a bright flaming light soaring skywards. So high in the end that it seemed as if she was touching the sky. Angels were all around and together they went to heaven. The little fir tree's wish was fulfilled after all!

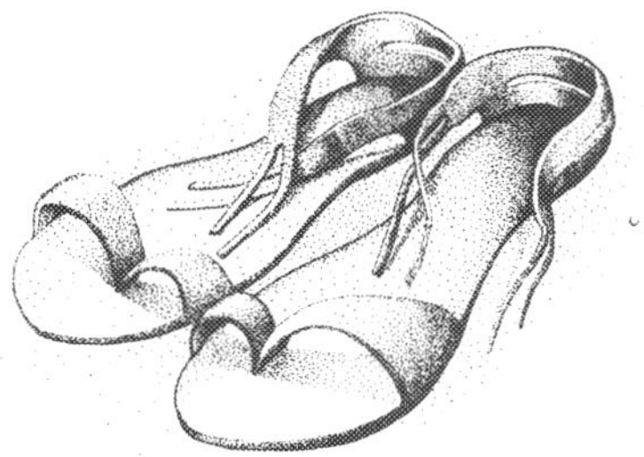

Colour – *purple*

What are we celebrating?

Lent is the time of preparation for the great events of Holy Week, Good Friday and Easter.

A time for:

- growing as Christians;
- recognizing the cost of following Jesus;
- understanding our need to be forgiven;
- self-discipline.

The word Lent comes from an old English word *(lengten)* which meant spring. This is when the days lengthen and the sunshine reveals cobwebs, dust and clutter, so we spring-clean our homes. For Christians, Lent is the opportunity for a spiritual spring-clean. Lent has traditionally been a time of fasting, prayer and self-denial. We think of the forty days Jesus spent in the wilderness, facing temptation and working out how to fulfil his godly mission. This led to him 'setting his face like flint' (Luke 9.51) and making his final journey to Jerusalem to confront the power structures, both religious and political.

Nowadays few Christians observe strict Lenten fasts but, happily, some of the customs remain. It may even be appropriate for some to be re-introduced! Lent is still an important time for prayer and spiritual renewal. Many people share in house groups, often with people from a variety of churches within their area.

Shrove Tuesday and **Ash Wednesday** mark the beginning of the season. **Mothering Sunday** (or Refreshment Sunday) comes in the middle, as a family break from the discipline. Towards the end comes **Palm Sunday**, which leads us into Holy Week with its highs and lows for the people, the disciples and Jesus.

What are the traditions?

❊ The Church's **traditional colour** is *purple*.

❊ **Shrove Tuesday**:

- pancake day, when rich foods were eaten up;
- carnivals (*Mardi Gras* – Fat Tuesday), still celebrated in many parts of the world.

❊ **Ash Wednesday**:

- confession;
- beginning of fast (Sundays in Lent are not fast days);
- using ashes to mark a cross on people's foreheads.

❊ **Mothering Sunday**:

- girls who had left home to work as servants used to travel home to visit their mothers;

- the girls would bake simnel cake to show their new skills to their mothers;
- recognition of 'Mother Church'.

❊ **Palm Sunday**:

- re-enacting Jesus' entry into Jerusalem;
- giving out palm crosses;
- waving palm branches.

What stories lead us in?

❊ **Lent:**

- Jonah 3.4-8
  (The need for repentance)
- Matthew 4.1-11
  (Jesus is tempted)
- Mark 8.34
  (Jesus challenges his followers)

❊ **Mothering Sunday:**

- Genesis 18.1-15
  (Sarah laughs when told she will become a mother)
- 2 Kings 4.1-7
  (Elijah helps a widow)

❊ **Palm Sunday:**

- Zechariah 9.9
  (The expected king comes in humility)

What can we do to prepare?

❊ Decide to live more **simply.** Discuss the options as a family.

❊ Make a **desert tray**. Cover the base of a tray or plastic box with a layer of sand. Add some stones, cacti and/or bare twigs.

❊ Make a **French Lenten calendar**. Trace the nun shape on page 28 onto card, then colour it in and cut it out. Be very careful not to lose any of her feet! Hang the 'nun' up, using string or thread. At the end of each week in Lent, fold one foot out of sight until, at Easter, she has none at all.

❊ Make a **Greek Lenten calendar**, called a *kukaras,* from a potato and seven large feathers. Scrub a large potato and make a hole through the middle of it, using a skewer or thin knitting needle. Thread a piece of string through the hole and tie a knot at one end to prevent the potato slipping off the string. Stick seven large feathers into the potato. If you cannot find any, make your own out of paper and cocktail sticks. Count down to Easter by removing one feather at the end of each week in Lent.

❊ Set up a **display corner**. This could include:

- a Bible, open at a different passage each week;
- a 'sharing box' for collecting coins, for instance all 5p coins;
- an empty bowl, to symbolize fasting (along with a family decision to do something for Lent);
- a cactus, as a reminder that Lent is a desert journey.

Prayer and Reflection

(Use a bunch of snowdrops or daffodils as a focus for meditation)

Green-hearted winter snowdrop,
symbol of God's renewing love,
turn your face to the sun,
as the days lengthen
and he sets his face to go towards Jerusalem.
Pale yellow hosanna trumpet of spring,
accompany him on his journey,
and as your shining petals brighten our day,
help us to sense his presence in our darkness,
his suffering in the agony of the world.
Flower fragrance of anointed love,
fill our house, our hearts, our world,
with the life giving news of Easter.

(Kate McIlhagga)

Lent's a time for new beginnings,
Death to our selfishness, sadness and greed.
Let there be born in us new hope and kindness
Then we'll be ready for Easter indeed.

(Author unknown)

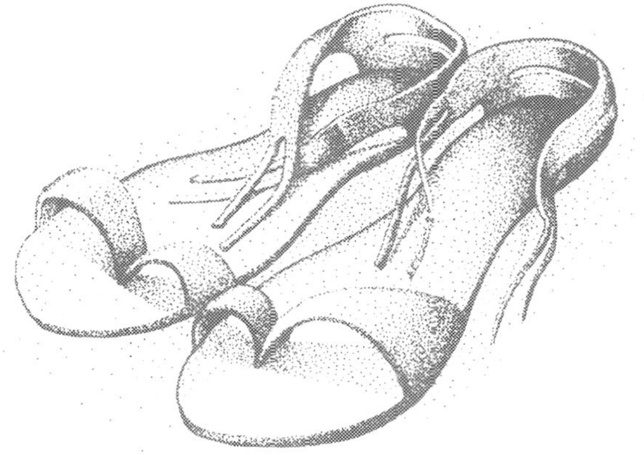

Use this template to make your French Lenten calendar.

What are we celebrating?

This is the last day before Lent, a time to 'clear the decks' by asking for forgiveness. (Shrove comes from an old English word which means penance.) This is also a time to have fun before the rigours of Lent.

Where are the stories?

Bible story

- Psalm 150
  (A song of praise)

Other stories

- *The Incredible Adventures of Professor Branestawm*
  'Pancake Day at Great Pagwell'
  Norman Hunter (Bodley Head)
- *Pancakes for breakfast*
  Tomie de Paola (Harcourt Brace)

What can we do to celebrate?

Do

Hold a carnival party

Dress up in fancy costumes or bright paper hats. Wear masks or paint your faces. Eat pancakes with savoury and sweet fillings. At the end, pray together and ring a bell to symbolize the start of Lent.

Make your home a carnival place

Decorate your home with crepe paper streamers. Play rough and tumble games. Reverse the roles of parent and child (for a restricted period!). Make up and act out a funny sketch. Put balloons outside your house.

Have a pancake race for everybody

All contestants should wear a headscarf and apron! Pancakes must be tossed three times during the race (in honour of the Trinity).

Eat

Sour milk pancakes:

110g self-raising flour
1 tblsp sugar
1 tsp salt
½ tsp bicarbonate of soda
1 beaten egg
240ml sour milk
oil for cooking

Beat together all the ingredients until the batter is smooth. Fry, using as little oil as possible.

Doughnuts

This is another way of using up eggs and fat.

Cakes and nuts

These are traditionally eaten in Germany and Switzerland on Shrove Tuesday

Plant

Put an amaryllis in a pot, to be ready for Easter.

Sing

(to the tune of *Frère Jacques*):

Mix a pancake
Stir it well
Put it in the basin
Stir it well

Cook a pancake

Fry it well
Till it's brown and yellow
Fry it well

Toss a pancake
Catch it well
Hold the handle tightly
Catch it well

Eat a pancake
Do it well
On a Shrove Tuesday
Do it well

What does it all add up to?

? Questions

Why should we have fun on this day in particular?

What does it say about the way we live for the rest of the year?

Traditionally people have given up luxuries for Lent. Should we be living more simply?

What can we do to take Lent more seriously?

☆ Insight

Joy and sadness are often intertwined. We must recognize the value of both if we are to live life to the full, in particular a Christian life. Lent and Easter give us an opportunity to do so.

➜ Action

Use this day to invite people you do not know well to share with you. Think of other ways in which you can show your care for others, for instance 'adopt' a grandparent.

Prayer and Reflection

Praise God!
In Sunday worship and daily work,
from the mountain tops and in the deep valleys
on holy ground and on common ground –
Praise God!

For the wonders of creation,
for human variety and gifts of creativity,
for freedom to worship in so many ways –
Praise God!

With trumpet and penny whistle, organ and ocarina,
with guitars and choirs, words and images,
with tambourines and dancing –
Praise God!

Let everything that has breath praise our Maker,
and let every breath be worship.
Praise God!
(Jan Pickard)

What are we celebrating?

This is the first day of Lent, a time to ask for and receive forgiveness.

Where are the stories?

Bible stories

- Matthew 4.1-11
  (Jesus is tempted)
- Matthew 6.5-18
  (Jesus teaches about prayer and fasting)

Other stories

- *Burglar Bill*
  Janet and Alan Ahlberg (Puffin)
- *I'm Sorry*
  Little Fish (Scripture Union)
- *I am David*
  Anne Holm (Methuen)
- *John Porter in Big Trouble*
  Tim Stafford (Lion)
- *Mabel and the Tower of Babel*
  John Ryan (Lion)
- *The Voyage of the Dawn Treader*
  CS Lewis (Collins/Lion)

What can we do to celebrate?

Do

Desert tray

Use the desert tray (see page 26) to tell the story of Jesus resisting the temptations.

Ashes

In some churches, the previous year's palm crosses are burned. The ash is used to make a cross on people's foreheads as a sign of forgiveness. At home, use ash, mixed with a little water, to make the sign of the cross on a window. As you do this, ask God to make you more like Jesus. Say the prayer, 'Help us, good Lord, to see you more clearly, love you more dearly, follow you more nearly, day by day.'

Spring cleaning

Take old clothes (if they are in good condition) to a charity shop. Put away children's pictures which have been around for a while, to allow space for new ones.

Marbles

Traditionally this game was played during Lent, beginning on Ash Wednesday.

Eat

Decide to eat more simply, perhaps having one main meal and restricting other meals to light snacks. Make the main meal special. Choose a special grace to use throughout Lent. Why not try lentils for Lent?

Here is a grace which you might wish to use:

> *'Loving God, to those who are hungry give bread, to us who have bread give the hunger for justice and fairness in the world.'* (From Latin America)

Listen

Gregorian chants

Solemn Melody. Vaughan Williams

Sing

'I'm sorry' (*Big Blue Planet*)

Pray

Say the Lord's Prayer together.

What does it all add up to?

Questions

Why was Jesus tempted?
Why did he have these particular temptations?
What does this story say to us today?
What must we do about it?

Insights

We are all tempted. We all make mistakes. We all need to ask for and receive forgiveness. We all need to be ready to forgive others. We need to take ourselves and others seriously – but not too seriously!

Actions

Consider whether there is something which you could do for each other. Perhaps choose a different course of action each week throughout Lent, e.g. giving extra hugs, turning off TV programmes which irritate others.

Prayer and Reflection

Light as a feather
A finger touched me,
Branded me cross-shaped,
Smudged me with ash.

Light as a feather
God's finger caressed me
With sign of forgiveness,
Marked me with love.

Light as a feather,
Penitent, shriven,
Signed with his life-mark
I go on my way.

(Ann Lewin)

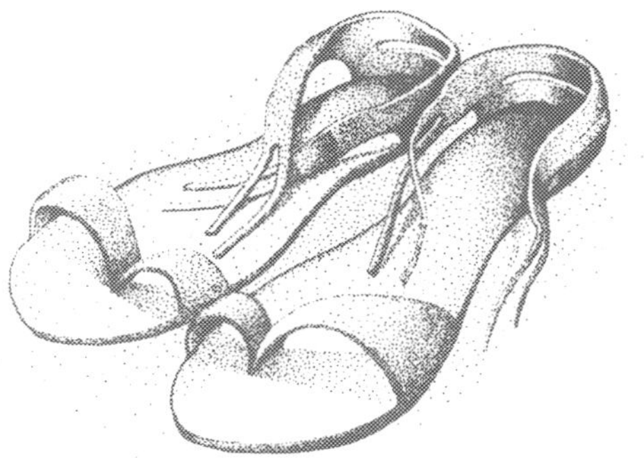

Mothering Sunday

What are we celebrating?

We escape briefly from the discipline of Lent to celebrate mothers. Also, drawing on old traditions, we celebrate Mother Church.

Where are the stories?

Bible stories

- 1 Samuel 1 and 2
  (Hannah's longing for a child and joy at Samuel's birth)
- Luke 2.41-52
  (Jesus and his family visit the Temple)
- Hosea 11.3-4
  (God loves the people of Israel like a mother)
- Isaiah 66.7-13
  (God loves Jerusalem like a mother)

Other stories

- *Not quite Mother's Day*
  Jenny Gubb (CHP/National Society)
- *Gemma, eat up*
  Jan Ormerod (Walker Books)
- *Bad mood bear*
  John Richardson (Beaver)

What can we do to celebrate?

Do

Take mum breakfast in bed or plan some other surprise.

Go to church together as a family.

Look

Spend a few minutes looking at the logo of the International Year of the Family:

What do you see in it? What does it say to you about being a family? Make a logo or crest for your family.

Make

Cards

Express your appreciation of the love and care shown by mothers and other caregivers.

Buttonholes

Use real or artificial flowers, and give them to mothers (and others).

A 'thank you' tree.

On luggage labels, write good things about each other. Hang the labels on a tree branch, stuck in a pot, along with enough sweets for everybody.

Danish hearts

You will need: paper of two different colours; scissors.

Cut an oblong from each colour of paper, and fold each oblong across its width. Cut a curved shape at the unfolded ends. Cut a central slit starting at the folded ends, and exactly the same length as the folded edges.

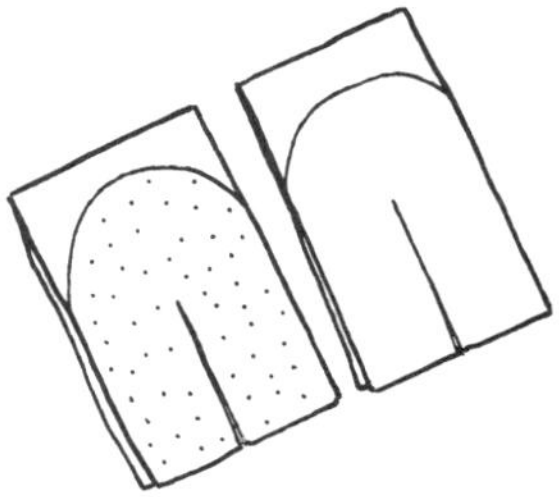

Weave the oblongs together as shown in the diagrams below:

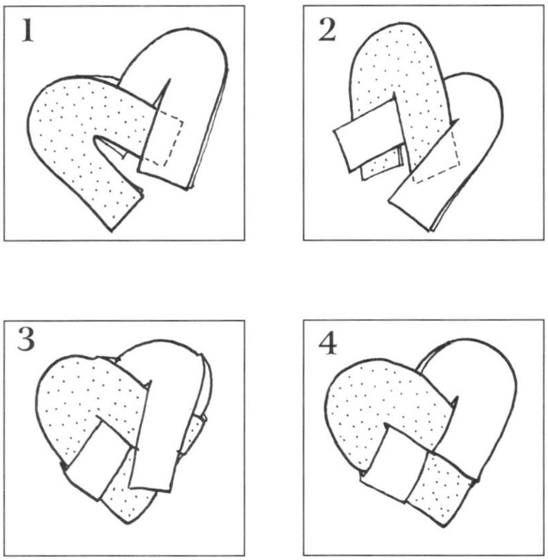

Hold the finished hearts in your hands and say this prayer:

'Dear God, thank you for people we can trust, especially ... Thank you that we can always trust you.'

Eat

A simnel cake:

225g margarine
225g sugar
450g self-raising flour
1 lemon
225g mixed dried fruit
some jam
2 packets marzipan

Cream margarine and sugar until fluffy. Add eggs, flour and flesh, juice and grated rind of lemon. Line a large cake tin with greased foil. Place half the mixture in the tin. Use a third of the marzipan to make a circle the size of the tin. Place it on the mixture in the tin. Add the rest of the mixture. Bake in a moderate oven for 90 minutes. Cover with greaseproof paper and bake for a further 30 minutes.

To decorate: make another marzipan circle to cover the top and roll out strips for the sides, using warmed jam as 'glue'. Brush with beaten egg and place under a grill until toasted. Decorate as you wish.

Hug

Give each other a special hug today.

Think

What do mothers do?

How is the Church like a mother?

What do you want to say in love and gratitude to your mother? What do you want to say to God? Are they similar things? Give each member of the family a flower. Put the flowers in a vase as you say a short prayer of thanks. Place the vase in the Lent corner or where you will all see it.

Sing

'God, you hold me, like a mother' (*Big Blue Planet*)

'At half past three we go home to tea' (*Someone's singing Lord*)

'He's got the whole world in his hands'

What does it all add up to?

? Questions

Is your church really like a mother? Is your church really like a family?

Why are families not always happy? Where is God in all that?

How can families celebrate Mothering Sunday in a world of commercialism?

☆ Insight

Love is at the heart of healthy family life, and where love is, God is.

➜ Action

Say thank you (and sorry) more often – to each other and to God.

Prayer and Reflection

Loving God
You are Father and Mother to us;
Our life begins in you.
You chose to make your home among us.
You sent your Son to be one with us,
And your Spirit to be with us for ever.
Bless this home
and your people who live here.
Be here today,
as you were yesterday.
Be here tomorrow.
Be our shelter,
our walls to protect us.
Be our windows;
let us see the world through you.
Be our warmth,
to share with all who come in
and all who go forth.
(Paul Leingang)

God, you hold me, like a mother,
Safely on her knee.
God, you hold me, like a mother,
Close to you but free.
(Andrew Pratt)

Palm Sunday

What are we celebrating?

We remember Jesus coming in triumph to Jerusalem, the religious and political capital. He is greeted as a king, but he rides on a donkey. The crowds are full of happiness, but Jesus cries over the city. The crowds live for today, but Jesus is only too aware of the danger in store.

Where are the stories?

Bible stories

- Luke 19.28-38
  (Jesus' entry into Jerusalem)
- Matthew 23.37
  (Jesus loves the people of Jerusalem as a hen gathers her chicks)

Other stories

- *Donkey's Glory*
  Nan Goodall (Mowbray)

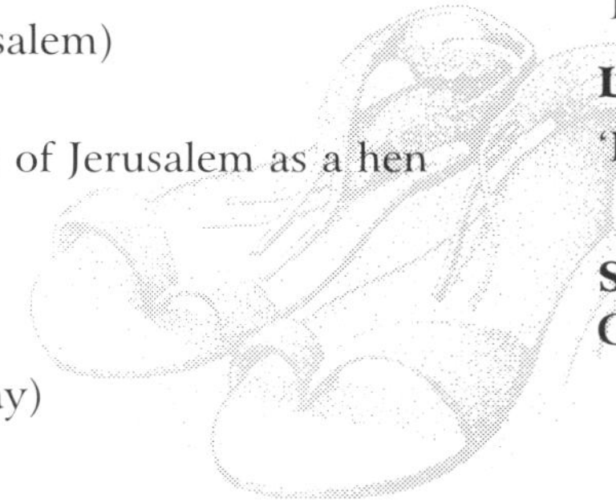

Looking ahead

What happened on Palm Sunday triggered Jesus' confrontation of the power groups in Jerusalem. He followed his triumphal entry by overturning the tables in the Temple (Luke 19.45-46) and by teaching pointedly in response to questions (Luke 20 and 21). All these actions inflamed the authorities. Look ahead to the Jerusalem city map in **Jesus dying and rising** (page 41).

What can we do to celebrate?

Play

Stick the tail on the donkey

Play this game to remember that donkeys are often seen as figures of fun.

Sing

'Hosanna, hosanna, shout hosanna to the king' (*Big Blue Planet*)

'We have a king who rides a donkey' (*Someone's singing Lord*)

'Riding on a donkey into town' (*Jerusalem Joy*)

Listen

'Hosanna' from *Jesus Christ, Superstar*. Tim Rice/Andrew Lloyd Webber

Sow

Cress

Sprinkle cress seeds on damp cotton wool spread over an upturned bowl (as they do in Poland). This will grow into a green hill in time for Good Friday and be ready to eat in egg sandwiches on Easter Day.

Collect

Pick some pussy willow and catkins to decorate the house.

Make

Chicks from bread dough

Form some of the dough into a little bun. Pinch out a beak and poke in raisins for eyes. Cook it. Decorate with ribbons etc. Alternatively, make a large mother hen-shaped loaf with baby chicks.

Posters

Make posters or placards saying what you think about Jesus e.g. 'Jesus is ACE'. Where will you display them?

A redemption calendar for Holy Week

You will need: a large sheet of paper; pens, pencils or crayons; scissors; tape or glue.

On the paper, draw an Ark shape with seven windows and a set of double doors:

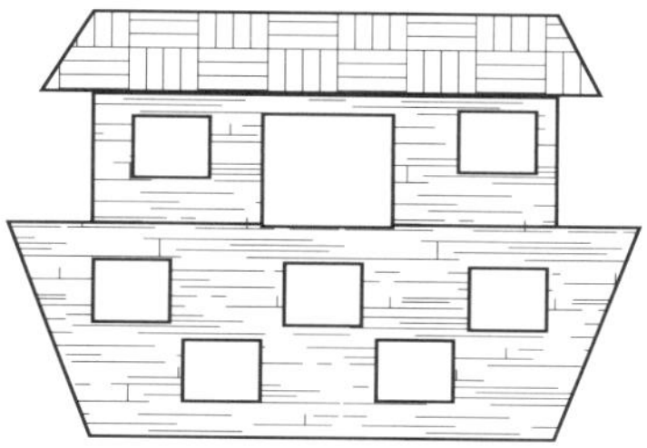

Cut around three sides of each of the windows and doors, so that they can be folded open when the time comes. Mark the seven windows with the days of the week from Palm Sunday to Holy Saturday. Mark the double doors 'Easter Sunday'. Draw or find an appropriate picture for each day of the week, or copy the pictures on the right. Make the pictures slightly larger than the doors in the Ark. Use tape or glue to fix each picture in place behind the appropriate door. Each day of the week, open the appropriate door.

What does it all add up to?

? Questions

Why did Jesus have to be so humble?

How can people be so fickle and unreliable?

Why was Jesus sad when he looked at Jerusalem?

☆ Insights

Power does not always come through a show of strength.

➜ Actions

Think about how you each use power in your family. Find ways of allowing different people to take the lead at different times.

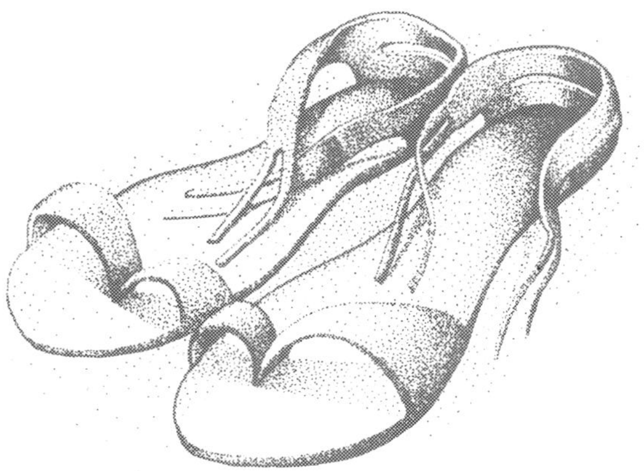

Prayer and Reflection

Snaffled my donkey, he did – good luck to him! –
Rode him astride, feet dangling, near scraping the ground.
Gave me the laugh of my life when I first seen them,
Remembering yesterday – you know, how Pilate come
Bouncing along the same road, only that horse of his
Big as a bloody house and the armour shining
And half Rome trotting behind. Tight-mouthed he was,
Looking like he owned the world.
Him and my little donkey! Ha – laugh? –
I thought I'd kill myself when he first started.
So did the rest of them. Gave him a cheer
Like he was Caesar himself, only more hearty:
Tore off some palm-twigs and followed shouting,
Whacking the donkey's behind... Then suddenly
We see his face.
The smile had gone, and somehow the way he sat
Was different – like he was much older – you know –
Didn't want to laugh no more.
(Clive Sansom)

Christ is coming, Christ is coming,
On a donkey, on a donkey,
Hosanna, Hosanna,
We wave our palm branches.
(Lothian Road Church Primary School)

Colours – *purple, black and white or gold*

What are we celebrating?

We enter into the passion, death and resurrection of Jesus.

A time for:

- remembering and praying;
- remembering and asking for forgiveness;
- remembering and waiting;
- rejoicing, dancing and singing.

In the four days of Easter, the story moves quickly and, for the disciples, the mood changes dramatically. On **Maundy Thursday** Jesus shares the Passover with them. For him there is foreboding; for them it is like any other special meal, enjoyed in the present, but without any understanding of its meaning. Afterwards, when the disciples looked back (as they talked about the events of the evening) they began to discover its significance.

Good Friday is when the pace quickens. Events move beyond the disciples' control, from saying they would never leave Jesus to denying that they ever knew him or running away in terror. Meanwhile, Jesus is tried, sentenced and condemned to death. A few of his disciples return in great fear, to be there at the last.

We, as his disciples today, try to be with Jesus in his suffering, acknowledging our lack of understanding, our guilt, fear, betrayal – and love. At the same time we recognize, with the benefit of hindsight, the huge significance of the events being played out before us. So we celebrate this day as a day set apart to be holy.

For the disciples **Holy Saturday** must have been the blackest day of all. It seemed like the end of all their hopes. It is important for us to remember their despair as we wait for Easter Day.

Then comes **Easter Day** – Christ is risen. Let us celebrate!

What are the traditions?

- The Church's **traditional colours** are *purple* for **Maundy Thursday**, *black* for **Good Friday** and **Holy Saturday**, and *white* or *gold* for **Easter Day**.
- **Maundy Thursday:**
  - footwashing ceremony;
  - sharing the Passover meal;
  - giving out Maundy money.
- **Good Friday**:
  - hot cross buns;
  - special services and vigils to think about Jesus' death on the cross.

- ❋ **Holy Saturday**:
  - no specific traditional activities, but it is a day of waiting.
- ❋ **Easter Day**:
  - eggs, chocolate eggs, egg rolling;
  - flowers, especially daffodils and lilies;
  - simnel cake;
  - new life;
  - reaffirming Baptismal promises.

What stories lead us in?

- ❋ **Maundy Thursday:** Exodus 12.21-28 (The first Passover)
- ❋ **Good Friday**: Isaiah 52.13 - 53.9 (God's suffering servant)
- ❋ **Holy Saturday**: Psalm 40 (God is faithful)
- ❋ **Easter Sunday:** Romans 8.35-39 (Jesus shows us God's love)

What can we do to prepare?

- ❋ Use the **Jerusalem city map** (see page 41). Match the pictures to the numbers and the Bible references.
- ❋ Use the **desert tray** or prepare a corner of the garden or a planter to build up scenes for this season.

Prayer and Reflection

Carol for Holy Week, to the tune of 'The Twelve Days of Christmas'

On the day of Good Friday
My true love gave to me
His own self upon a bare tree.

On the Saturday that followed
My true love gave to me
Rest after pain
And his own self upon a bare tree.

On the first day of Easter
My true love gave to me
Life, new life,
Rest after pain
And his own self upon a bare tree.

All the days after Easter
My true love gives to me
Grace for my living,
Joy in my giving,
Comfort in sorrow,
Strength for tomorrow,
Love without end –
His risen light,
Life, new life,
Rest after pain
And his own self upon a bare tree.

(Pamela Egan)

Jerusalem city map

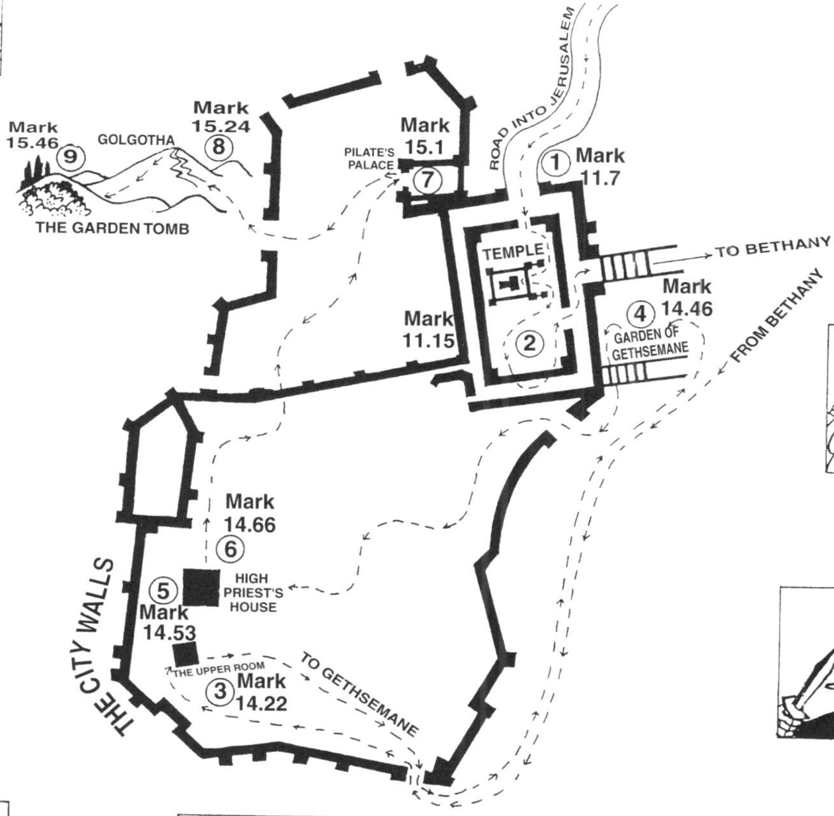

Maundy Thursday

What are we celebrating?

The night before the crucifixion of Jesus, he and his disciples ate together; he prayed alone in the Garden of Gethsemane and Judas betrayed him.

Where are the stories?

Bible stories

- Mark 14.12-52
  (The events of Maundy Thursday)
- John 13.2-17
  (Jesus washes the disciples' feet)

Other stories

- *Dogger*
  Shirley Hughes (Red Fox)
- *The Lion, the Witch and the Wardrobe*
  CS Lewis (Collins/Lion) or BBC Video
- *Haffertee's First Easter*
  Janet and John Perkins (Lion)

What can we do to celebrate?

Make

Bread

Shape the dough into a cross or a crown of thorns.

A Maundy bag

Make a small draw-string bag, to remind you of Judas' bag with thirty pieces of silver and of the British monarch distributing Maundy money. Alternatively, decorate envelopes.

Sing

'From hand to hand' (*Big Blue Planet*)

'Judas, Judas, what have you done?' (*Story Song*)

Listen

St Matthew Passion. Bach

Jesus Christ, Superstar. Tim Rice and Andrew Lloyd Webber

Give

Gifts

Take a Maundy bag with a small gift to someone who is ill or alone.

Maundy money

Put in Maundy bags a collection of new or polished coins, one of each denomination. Place them on the supper table, one for each person present.

Do

Footwashing

Be kind to someone, remembering Jesus washing the feet of the disciples.
Wash each other's feet or hands.

Bread and wine

Put bread on a plate and wine (or red grape juice) in a glass. Place them beside a cross on a table or windowsill where you can see them and be reminded of Jesus' last supper with his disciples.

Eat and remember

Love feast

Use the home-made bread as part of a love feast.

Matzos

These are similar to the unleavened bread that Jesus and the disciples shared.

Passover meal

Roast a joint of lamb with garlic and herbs. Eat with pitta bread, remembering the Passover meal. Vegetarians might have nut roast with herb stuffing.

What does it all add up to?

? Questions

Why are the events of Maundy Thursday important for us today?

Why did Jesus wash the feet of the disciples? What does this mean for us?

Why did the disciples let Jesus down? How do we let people down? How do we let Jesus down?

☆ Insights

We can remember Jesus in a special way through the sharing of bread and wine.

Jesus came to serve and help us.

➜ Actions

Make space for a special time of quiet as a family.

Say prayers of repentance, each person thinking for themselves (though not sharing aloud) about times when they have let someone down and, in doing so, have let Jesus down.

Prayer and Reflection

Each family
At table meets;
From home and school
Each other greet:
A time to talk,
A time to eat,
Welcome and love
Each day repeat.

Some tables full;
Some sadly bare:
To sacrifice
Who now will dare?
Then, giving thanks,
Begin to share,
Since Christ the Lord
Invites our care.

We gather round
A table here.
We meet as friends,
The Lord is near.
With bread and wine
We celebrate:
By sign and word
Christ's love relate.
(Donald Hilton)

Good Friday

What are we celebrating?

Jesus allowed himself to be put to death. The story of Good Friday is central to the Christian faith but can be very difficult to share with children. Try to find ways of doing this which are appropriate to your family.

Where are the stories?

For this day there are several incidents which make up the whole story, told in different ways, emphasizing different details, in the four Gospels. They are all listed for you to explore as you wish.

Bible stories

- Matthew 26.57 - 27.61
- Mark 14.53 - 15.47
- Luke 22.54 - 23.56
- John 18.28 - 19.42

Other stories

- *The Easter Story*
  Brian Wildsmith (Oxford)
- *The Three Trees*
  Trad., retold by Angela Elwell Hunt (Lion)
- *The Lion, the Witch and the Wardrobe*
  CS Lewis (Collins/Lions) or BBC Video
- *The Happy Prince*
  Oscar Wilde (Puffin)
- *The Bamboo Tree* (See page 47)

What can we do to celebrate?

Make

An Easter garden
Add a green hill, three crosses and a tomb to your desert tray. Make a path of stones from the cross to the tomb.

A cross
Make a cross using twigs and string. Put it where you can see it and remember Jesus' love.

Place-cards
Make a place-card, in the shape of a cross, for each member of the family. Use them at family meals over the weekend.

A crown of thorns
Use flexible twigs to make a crown of thorns. Hang it over the cross you have made.

Hot cross buns
Make or buy hot cross buns.

Look

Cress
Is the cress you sowed on Palm Sunday now a green hill?

Pictures
Look at paintings, sculpture or other representations of Jesus on the cross.
Go into a church and look at stained glass windows and the Stations of the Cross.

Eat
Hot cross buns.

Collect

Find pictures, headlines and short articles from newspapers and magazines about pain and suffering, loss and distress. Make them into a cross shape and use them as a focus for prayer.

Sing

'There is a green hill far away'

'When I survey the wondrous cross'

'He is dying' ('Hosanna, hosanna', *Big Blue Planet*)

'Two long pieces of wood' (*Big Blue Planet*)

'The Servant King'

Listen

Messiah. Handel

The Crucifixion. Stainer

Jesus Christ Superstar. Tim Rice/Andrew Lloyd Webber

Godspell. Stephen Schwartz

Go out

Take a quiet walk in the countryside or a park. Notice the trees in particular.

Remember

Put a cross in the window.

Have quiet family prayers at 12 noon or 3.00 p.m., the time of the Crucifixion.

What does it all add up to?

? **Questions**

Why did Jesus' crucifixion happen?

Was it inevitable?

Did it have to happen?

Were the people afraid of goodness, of new ideas, or what?

Did they behave differently because they were part of a crowd?

Why did the religious leaders behave the way they did?

What would we have done if we had been there?

What are the implications for us today?

☆ **Insights**

'God loved the world so much that he gave his only Son, so that everyone who believes in him may not die but have eternal life' (John 3.16).

Today there is much evil and cruelty in the world. When we let God down, we cause him pain. God is still at work reconciling the world to himself.

➜ **Actions**

Consider what you should do for someone else.

Look afresh at what Jesus means for us.

Prayer and Reflection

There is a man with back bent in pain,
The weight he bears a heavy cross,
As people call and jeer.
Beads of sweat and blood mingle,
And a crown of thorns mocks.
His face a portrait of pain.
The man hangs calm and still
The weight he bears the people's sins
As people cry and weep.
The world is black as night,
But radiance lights his face.
His face is a portrait of peace
For all the world to share.
(Amy, aged 10)

If you use this story, illustrate it with a piece of bamboo split lengthwise.

The Bamboo Tree stood tall and straight, holding up its head proudly because it knew that it was the master's favourite tree. When the master walked in his garden the Bamboo would bow its proud head in greeting.

One day the master stood before the Bamboo and said, 'Bamboo, Bamboo, I must cut you down.' 'Cut me down! Oh no, master! No!' 'Yes,' said the master. 'You cannot serve me unless you let me cut you down.' The Bamboo bowed its proud head, saying sadly, 'Very well, master, cut me down if that is the only way I can serve you.' 'That is the only way,' said the master. And so he cut the Bamboo down.

The next day the master stood looking down at the proud Bamboo Tree lying on the ground, its trunk long and straight and its branches spread out. 'Bamboo, Bamboo,' said the master, 'I must cut off your branches.' 'All of them?' cried the Bamboo. 'All of them,' said the master, 'or you cannot serve me.' 'Very well,' sighed the Bamboo, 'Cut all my branches off, for I would serve you!' So the master cut off all the branches.

The Bamboo lay alone for a time thinking sadly of all its lost beauty, and wondering what else the master had in store for it. Presently the master returned and said, 'Bamboo, Bamboo, you have a fine, strong, straight trunk. I must split you in half from top to bottom and take out your pith.' 'Oh no, no, master!' wailed the Bamboo. 'I shall die if you do that. I will serve any way I can, but do not split me!' 'Bamboo, you cannot serve me if I do not split you in two and take out your pith.' 'As you will, master,' whispered the Bamboo. So the master split the Bamboo from end to end and took out all the pith. Then he laid the two halves of the trunk end to end and fastened them firmly together. One end he laid at the mouth of a little spring of water which bubbled out of the ground and lost itself among the moss and stones. The other end he placed in his rice field which was parched and dry. Soon the clear spring water was running from the spring down the channel made by the Bamboo trunk into the dry rice field, bringing refreshment to the drooping, dying plants.

So the Bamboo died and brought new life to the master's rice field. The rice grew tall and strong and brought life to many hungry people.

Holy Saturday

What are we celebrating?

We look back with regret, but look forward in anticipation. So it is a day of waiting and of preparation.

Where are the stories?

Bible stories

- John 19.38-42
  (Joseph and Nicodemus put Jesus' body in the tomb)
- Luke 23.54-56
  (The women prepare and wait)

Other stories

- *Charlotte's Web*
  EB White (Puffin)
- *The Enterprising Grub* (see page 51)
- *Horton the elephant*
  Dr Seuss
- *Donkey's Glory*
  Nan Goodall (Mowbray)

What can we do to celebrate?

Make

Cake

Have an Easter cake (maybe a Simnel cake, see the recipe on page 34). Decorate it with eleven balls of marzipan (for the 'faithful' disciples) and an Easter chick.

Easter biscuits:

250g self-raising flour
pinch of salt
125g soft margarine
125g sugar
1 level tsp cinnamon
65g currants
1 egg

Rub the margarine into the flour. Add the sugar, cinnamon and salt, then the currants. Add the egg. At first, it feels as if the mixture won't stick together, but if you keep working it with your hands, you'll find that it will. When the mixture is pliable, roll it out very thinly on a floured surface, and cut it into biscuit rounds. Use an upturned glass if you don't have cutters. Bake at gas mark 5 or 6 or 170° C until golden brown. (Check after 12-15 minutes.)

If you wish, you could cut out rabbit shapes and dab icing on to make the tail and an eye, or you could ice round biscuits and put sugar-coated chocolate eggs on so that they resemble nests. But they're good just plain!

Eggs

Make Easter nests from melted chocolate and rice krispies. Fill with tiny eggs.

Decorate hardboiled eggs.

Make marshmallow Easter eggs using the following recipe:

Marshmallow Easter eggs

1 cup icing sugar
flour
melted chocolate
EITHER 2 dessert spoons gelatine, 1 egg white, 1 cup sugar and 1 cup cold water
OR 1 packet jelly and 1 cup boiling water

EITHER soften the gelatine in the cold water, add the sugar and boil for 8 minutes then cool. Beat the egg white until stiff, fold in the icing sugar, then slowly pour it into the cooled gelatine mixture. Beat until thick, for about 3 minutes.

OR dissolve the jelly with the boiling water. Boil for 8 minutes without stirring, then leave to cool slightly. Add the icing sugar and beat until stiff, for about 3 minutes.

Put a pile of flour on a plate and make indentations in it with the back of a tablespoon, and pour the mixture into the hollows. You need to work fairly fast – it sets in 15 minutes.

Lift the shapes out and pair them up to make egg shapes. Leave them overnight in the fridge or freezer. Dip them in melted chocolate and leave to set again.

Makes about 10 eggs.

A Paschal Candle

You will need: a thick candle (not less than 3-4cm in diameter) in white or natural colour; 5 coloured mapping pins; decorations such as stick-on stars or transfers; wax crayons (optional).

Stick the mapping pins into the candle to make a cross shape. Put the top pin approximately one third of the way down the candle, so that it can safely stay lit throughout your meal.

Then add the decorations. Or, if you are more adventurous, carefully carve a design into the candle and then add colour with melted wax crayons. This will need considerable care as heating the wax crayons can become extremely messy. However the finished product can be very effective.

Wait

Desert tray

Seal the tomb in the Easter garden.

Dormant life

Gather a collection of items which appear dead but have life within (e.g. eggs, chrysalis, sunflower seeds, matches, candles, flower bulbs).

Prepare

Place a bare branch or twig in a large pot, ready to make an Easter tree tomorrow.

Set up an Easter egg hunt (but keep it a surprise for the children).

Listen

'I waited for the Lord' from *Elijah*. Mendelssohn

Sing

'Kindle a flame' (see page 77)

Do

Put the Paschal candle in a bowl of sand.

Surround it with other candles. In the dark, light

the Paschal candle. Light the others from it, singing 'Kindle a flame' (see page 77).

Pray

Set aside time (even just a few minutes) for everyone to be quiet and still. Think about the Easter story. Meet afterwards and say a prayer together.

What does it all add up to?

Questions

How do you feel about this day?

What is good about having to wait?

Has preparing for Easter Day made you think more about what it means?

How important is the experience of sadness to our understanding of joy?

Insights

When we accept the reality of the present we are better able to face the future.

The sharpness of death prepares us for the experience of new life.

Actions

Think of other times when it is good to wait and think – and plan to use them.

Prayer and Reflection

Today or tomorrow I will be here
Waiting
Waiting for something:
An answer,
An answer to all my questions.
So far they've all been lies.
They seem the truth until I discover something new,
Something I was not aware of before.
But maybe there isn't an answer,
I mean, one only,
Because it seems the way you look at it, the answer changes,
The reason changes
And everything is seen in a different light.

(Anon, 14)

When I'm crying deep inside,
Harder than I've ever cried,
Help me to remember, you are
Loving me.

(Joy Webb)

'Gritty' Grub they called him, and he certainly did look gritty! There he lay at the bottom of the pond in the mud, looking rather like a dead twig with little bits of stone and sand sticking to it. All the other pond creatures were a bit sorry for him because they could swim about, sometimes down to the dark depths amongst the weeds and sometimes right to the top where they could see the sunlight shining on the surface of the water. Poor old Gritty could only crawl about on his strange little legs at the bottom. 'Poor old Gritty Grub,' they said, 'What a pity he can't swim! He'll have to spend all his life at the bottom in the mud.' 'Unless he crawled up a stalk of weed,' suggested somebody. 'Oh, he'd never do that,' said a tadpole, wriggling his long tail. 'He'd get stuck and then fall to the bottom again!' and he swam off to the top of the pond to get a breath of air.

But one day, the pond creatures all had a surprise. 'Just look at Gritty Grub!' said the minnow, 'He's actually climbing a stalk!' And sure enough Gritty Grub was climbing, very slowly, out of the mud and up a strong stalk of water weed. Everyone watched to see how soon he would get stuck and fall back into the mud. But they waited a long time! Gritty didn't get stuck and he didn't fall back into the mud; he went on climbing, climbing, climbing!

'What's he going to do when he gets to the top?' asked the minnow. 'Crawl or fall back again, I suppose,' said the water beetle. But he didn't do either! After a long slow climb, Gritty Grub's head came out of the water and he drew a big breath of fresh air. He was very tired, but his journey wasn't finished yet. He crawled on until he was right out of the water and safely on a leaf. He lay there and rested in the spring sunshine. It warmed and dried him and he began to feel better. He still looked like a bit of dead twig with grit sticking to it.

All the pond people watched as he disappeared out of the water. 'Wherever has he gone?' they asked, 'He'll die up there!' And they waited for him to return, but he never did! Everyone in the pond thought that was the end of him. But was it?

It was a wonderful day for Gritty Grub when he crawled out of the water. As he lay resting on the leaf, a beautiful creature with white wings fluttered down beside him. 'Hello, brother' said Whitewings. 'Did you say "brother"?' asked Gritty. 'You can't be my brother. You're nothing like me! You have beautiful white wings and a shiny body and I'm just an ugly old grub! Oh dear, I don't know why I came.' 'You will!' said Whitewings, 'Just you wait!' As he spoke, Gritty felt something strange happen! It felt as though his gritty coat had split all down the back. And that was just what had happened! 'There you are! I told you so!' said Whitewings. Gritty wriggled and as he did so two rather damp creased wings appeared through the split in his coat. 'When the sun has dried those wings of yours they'll be just like mine and you'll be able to fly about like me!' said Whitewings. 'Have a look at yourself in the water.' Gritty crept to the edge of the leaf and peeped over, and there in the water, which was like a mirror, he saw not a gritty bit of twig, but a creature with white shining wings which were becoming more beautiful every minute as the sun dried them. The gritty coat was finished with and lay on the leaf until a little wave of water swept it off and it sank to the bottom of the pond. 'We'll have to give you a new name.' said Whitewings, 'You can't be called "Gritty" any more. How about Whitefeather? Come on, let's fly to that water lily.' And off they flew together. Gritty Grub had a beautiful new body and a new name and he was wonderfully happy. He forgot all about the mud at the bottom of the pond, and his old gritty coat. The pond creatures saw the Gritty Grub coat falling through the water. 'Here he comes,' they said. But when they looked they could see it was only the coat and Gritty wasn't there at all!

What are we celebrating?

We rejoice in the resurrection of Jesus, which is central to the Christian message.

Where are the stories?

Bible stories

The Gospels emphasize the appearance of the Risen Jesus to different people.

- Matthew 28.1-10
- Mark 16.1-8
- Luke 24.1-43
- John 20.1-29; 21.1-19

Other stories

- *The Lion, the Witch, and the Wardrobe*
  CS Lewis. (Collins/Lions) or BBC Video
- *The Bamboo Tree* (see page 47)
- *The Very Hungry Caterpillar*
  Eric Carle (Puffin)
- *Badger's Parting Gifts*
  Susan Varley (Random Century)
- *Petook*
  Caryl Houselander and Tomie de Paola (Burns and Oates)
- *The Selfish Giant*
  Oscar Wilde (Puffin)

What can we do to celebrate?

Do

Desert tray

Roll away the stone from the tomb of the Easter garden.

Add flowers to the Easter garden.

Candle

Light the Paschal candle.

Church

Go to church!

Easter eggs

Have the Easter egg hunt.
Hang painted eggs on a tree branch.

Endings

Put a smile on the face of the Lenten nun.

Beginnings

Look at the amaryllis which you planted on Shrove Tuesday. Is it in flower?

New life

Go for a walk, looking for signs of new life.

Eat

Have decorated eggs for breakfast.
Enjoy the Easter goodies.
Cut the cress and make egg and cress sandwiches.

Say

Grace before lunch.

One person should say, 'Alleluia, the Lord is risen'. Everyone should then reply, 'Alleluia, he is risen indeed'.

Listen

'Hallelujah chorus'. *Messiah.* Handel

Russian Easter Festival Overture. Rimsky-Korsakov

'Alleluia', from *Six Songs.* Mozart

Sing

'Hosanna, hosanna' (*Big Blue Planet*)
'After darkness, light' (*Hymns and Psalms*)
'Two long pieces of wood' (*Big Blue Planet*)
'Halle, halle, halle' (*Wild Goose*)

What does it all add up to?

? Questions

What is it about Easter that makes it even more important than Christmas? (Remember the Epiphany Tree, page 24.)

What stories are there in your family that speak of new life?

☆ Insights

In remembering the events of the past we celebrate the reality of the present.

Jesus is alive today!

➜ Actions

Plant some sunflower seeds in the garden or a tub. As you do so, remember Jesus' words in John 12.24: 'I am telling you the truth: a grain of wheat remains no more than a single grain unless it is dropped into the ground and dies. If it does die, then it produces many grains.' This process is an illustration of how God works through us.

Prayer and Reflection

How can he tell
It is the hour
To burst the shell
And overpower
The cold hard prison walls?
It is the Easter wonder!

Into the sun,
The clean fresh air;
His life begun,
He stands to stare,
For Spring is all around,
It is the Easter wonder!

The trees and flowers
Are now new-dressed;
In sunshine hours
The birds build nests.
New life is all around.
It is the Easter wonder!

And from the tomb
Our Lord did rise,
Dispelling gloom;
Gave us the prize
Of everlasting life.
It is the Easter wonder.
(A. Elliott Cameron)

GOD LET LOOSE IN THE WORLD

Colours – white or gold and red

What are we celebrating?

God is available to us day by day.

A time for:

- celebrating God's love everywhere and in the lives of people;
- using symbols to express what we find difficult to say;
- beginning to recognize that God is not only vast and beyond our understanding but also near and within each of us.

In John Masefield's play *The Coming of Christ*, the Roman centurion in charge of Jesus' crucifixion presents his report to Pilate. Pilate's wife is very interested and asks, 'Where is he now? Is he dead?' The centurion replies, 'No, lady.' 'Well, where is he?' 'Let loose in the world, ma'am, where neither Roman nor Jew can stop him.'

From **Ascension Day** to **Trinity Sunday** we focus on the presence of the risen Christ and the power of the Holy Spirit. We celebrate the three persons of God – Father, Son, and Holy Spirit – coming to us in different ways.

What are the traditions?

❋ The Church's traditional colours are *white* or *gold* for **Ascension**, *red* for **Pentecost** and *white* or *gold* for **Trinity.**

❋ **Ascension Day**:

- in the past this was a public holiday;
- the blessing of the crops and the beating of the bounds;
- well-dressing, the decorating of village wells with pictures made of flower petals;
- the symbol for Ascension is a crown, representing the 'Coronation of the King of Kings'.

❋ **Pentecost:**

- the symbols are fire, wind and dove;
- the birthday of the Church;
- traditionally called Whitsun (White Sunday), the occasion for baptisms, when people came wearing white;
- in the north of England, the occasion for processions of witness and gatherings in parks for 'Whit Sings'.

❋ **Trinity:**

- the symbols – triangle, shamrock, three fishes – all reflect the 'threeness' of God;
- traditionally, ordinations of priests took place.

What stories lead us in?

- **Ascension:**
  - 2 Kings 2.1-12
    (Elijah hands his work on to his disciple and is taken up to heaven)
- **Pentecost:**
  - Genesis 1.1-2
    (The spirit of God was present at the beginning)
  - Joel 2.28-32
    (Prophecy of the coming of the spirit on all people)
  - Ezekiel 37
    (The Spirit bringing life to dry bones)
- **Trinity:**
  - Matthew 3.16
    (Jesus' baptism)

What can we do to prepare?

- Search for **signs** and **symbols** (e.g. road signs, T shirts, company logos). What do they represent? How effective are they? Why?
- Look around your church building for **Christian symbols**. What do they represent?
- Design a symbol or logo for your church.
- Watch the news or read a newspaper. Look out for examples of God's goodness at work in the world, e.g. the emergency services, aid workers, and any other cases of people helping others.
- Make a collage to show different ways in which God is at work in the world.

Prayer and Reflection

God has put a circle round us
Up and down and all around us
God has put a circle round us
Thank you, Lord.

Jesus came into the circle
Right in the middle of the circle
Jesus came into the circle
Thank you, Lord.

Jesus shows how much God loves us
Now and always, yes he loves us
Jesus shows how much God loves us
Thank you, Lord.

God has put a circle round us
By his Spirit all around us
God has put a circle round us
Thank you, Lord.
(Jenny Dann)

What are we celebrating?

We remember Jesus leaving his disciples to become one with God. The risen Jesus is no longer bound to earth's space and time.

Where are the stories?

Bible stories

- Luke 24.45-53
  (As Jesus leaves, he tells his disciples to wait in Jerusalem until the promised Holy Spirit comes)
- Acts 1.1-11
  (Jesus entrusts his mission to his disciples and leaves them)

Other stories

- *Wind and Fire*
  Susan Sayers and Arthur Baker (Kevin Mayhew)
- *The Snowman*
  Raymond Briggs (Hamish Hamilton)
- *Tim Walks*
  Rachel Anderson (CHP/NS)
- *The Happy Prince*
  Oscar Wilde (Penguin)
- *Footprints* meditation
  (widely available)

What can we do to celebrate?

Think

The symbol for the Ascension is a crown. What sort of king was Jesus when he lived on earth? Is he any different now?

Make

Crowns

Make and wear paper crowns to remember Jesus as king.

Balloons

Write an Ascension message (e.g. 'Up with Jesus!') on a helium balloon and let it go.

Eat

Share a picnic in a (safe) high place.

Do

Trust walk

Go for a walk in pairs, with one wearing a blindfold. The other directs and leads them around an obstacle course.

Up high

Climb a hill or tower and enjoy the view.

Sing

Jesus' love is very wonderful,
Jesus' love is very wonderful,
Jesus' love is very wonderful,
O wonderful love!

So high, you can't get over it,
So low, you can't get under it,
So wide, you can't get round it,
O wonderful love!

Listen

Theme music of *The Snowman* video (BBC)

Write

Send a letter to a friend or relative who lives a long way away.

What does it all add up to?

? Questions

Why does the Ascension matter?
What difference does it make to us?
How can we be God's witnesses? (See Acts 1.8)

☆ Insights

Jesus is no longer tied to one place or time. He is here now.
Jesus has taken our human experience into the Godhead.

➜ Actions

Plan how to show God's love in your neighbourhood, e.g. collect for Christian Aid, take a friend to church.

Prayer and Reflection

I wonder how you would do it nowadays?
Then, you took your eleven friends for a walk
And when you disappeared in the cloud
they knew you were saying goodbye to them.
They had to get used to the idea that they
weren't going to see you any more,
as they had done for nearly three years.
But they had your promise,
'Remember, I am with you always,
To the end of time.'
It's wonderful to know that you are around;
I don't have to go to a special place,
Or say particular words -
Or even feel in the right mood.
'I am with you always,' you said.
I hope I remember that – at least sometimes.
(Brother Kenneth & Sister Geraldine)

What are we celebrating?

Pentecost marks the coming of the Holy Spirit to the friends and followers of Jesus to give them power to do God's work.

Where are the stories?

Bible stories

- Joel 2.28-29
  (God's Spirit will come)
- Acts 2.1-13
  (The coming of the Holy Spirit)
- Acts 2.14-36
  (Peter preaching)
- Acts 2.37-47
  (What happened next)
- Acts 3.1-10
  (The healing of the man at the Beautiful Gate)

Other stories

- *The Windy Day* (*Teddy Horsley* series)
  Leslie J Francis and Nicola M Slee (NCEC)
- *Fabulous Beasts*
  (Macdonald Educational)
- *Wind and Fire*
  Susan Sayers and Arthur Baker (Kevin Mayhew)
- *The Wind Eye*
  Robert Westall (Puffin Plus)
- *The Big Fisherman*
  Lloyd C Douglas (Available from libraries)
- *The Burning Men*
  Stuart Jackman (Faber)

What can we do to celebrate?

Make

A paper windmill

You will need: a square of strong paper; a pair of compasses and a pencil; scissors; a pin; some paper; a straight stick.

Draw a small circle in the centre of the square of paper. Cut along the diagonals to the circle.

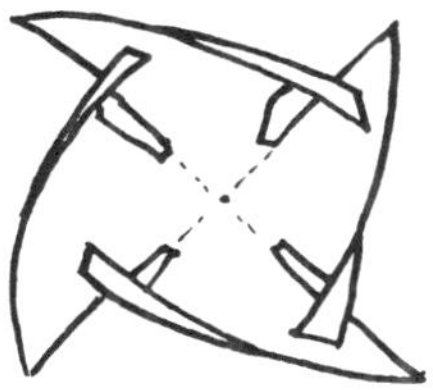

Bend over one corner of each leaf towards the centre.

Overlap each corner at the centre, and push the pin through all five layers.

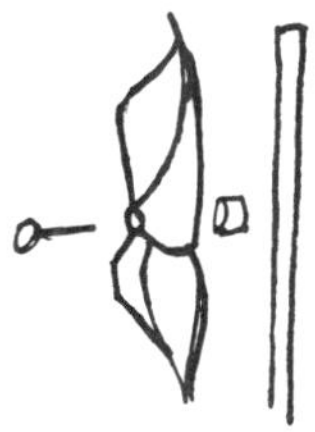

Make a paper collar and slip it over the pin. Push the pin into the stick.

Paper doves

You will need: paper; tissue paper; scissors; glue.

EITHER: Using the template on page 62, cut paper into dove shapes, using pieces of paper folded concertina-style for tails.

OR: Make 3-dimensional doves, using the following instructions:

Cut a circle of paper and fold it in half. Draw on wings, and cut a slit where indicated.

Pleat a rectangle of tissue paper. Pass it through the slit, open it out and glue the ends together.

Add eyes and a paper beak. Hang the dove up, or perch it on a twig.

A cake

Bake a cake in the shape of a dove.

A Pentecost mobile

Bring the symbols of Pentecost together to make a mobile. Put a dove in the centre, surrounding it with seven red and orange flames to represent the gifts of the Spirit (1 Corinthians 12.4-11). Hang it where it will move in a draught.

Do

'Wind' things

Fly a kite, blow bubbles, sail a yacht, blow up a bicycle tyre, pump bellows, wave streamers.

'Fire' things

Light sparklers, light a fire, have a bonfire.

Eat

Have a barbecue.

A birthday cake

Celebrate the birthday of the Church with a birthday cake. Decorate it with red and orange flames and one white candle.

Fiery food and clothes

Find something red to wear and eat flame-coloured food, e.g. tomatoes, carrots, peppers, oranges.

Sing

'Who can see the great wind blow?' (*Someone's singing Lord*)

'Colours of day' (*Come and Praise*)

'Like fireworks lighting up the night' (*Partners in Praise*)

Listen

Chariots of Fire

Firedance video

The wind, the crackle of a fire.

What does it all add up to?

Questions

Why is wind such a powerful symbol of the Spirit?

How can we be sure that something we cannot see or touch can be so powerful and important?

What does the symbol of fire mean for you?

Insight

Seeing is not always believing.

Actions

Choose one of the symbols we use for the Holy Spirit (wind, fire, dove). Look out for it in the next week. Does the Holy Spirit work in the same way?

Prayer and Reflection

Red sun shining down on me,
Warm and wonderful and free,
Lord Jesus, please fill us
With your light and energy.

Wild wind blowing fresh and strong,
Whipping all the leaves along,
Lord Jesus, please help us
Hear your power in its song.
(Doreen Newport)

A single flame may become a bush fire
A breath of wind may become a wild hurricane
The Holy Spirit is ever-present, but not in our control.
(Anon)

God as fire, send your spirit to us now,
Burn in us with cleansing power.
Come set alight your life in us,
Spirit, enter, as God of fire.
God the wind, send your spirit to us now,
Blow through us with stirring power.
Come, breathe your gifts on us today,
Spirit, enter, as God the wind.
God as dove, send your spirit to us now,
Comfort us with strength and power.
Come, fly with peace to all our hearts,
Spirit, enter, as God the dove.
(Judy Jarvis)

Use this template to make your paper doves, adding a pleated paper tail.

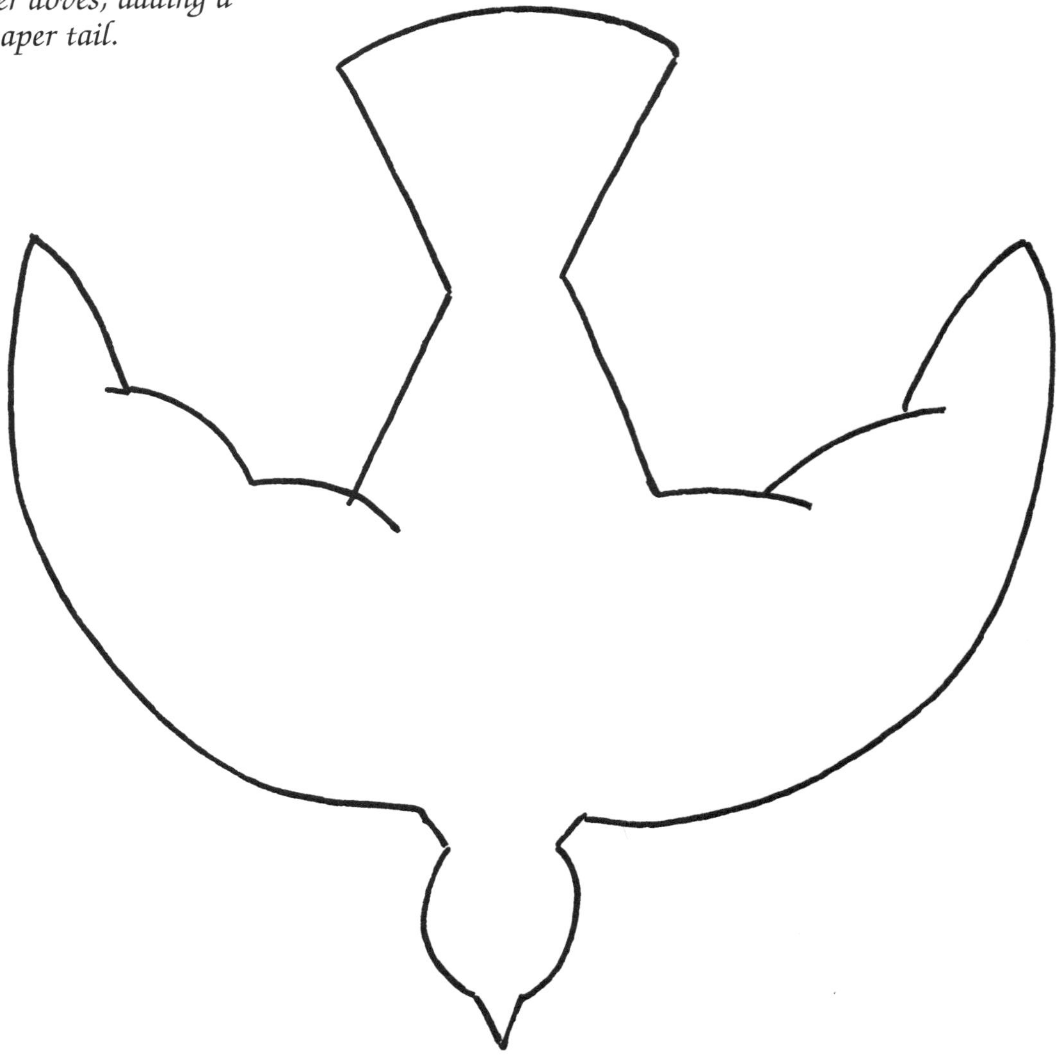

What are we celebrating?

Trinity Sunday brings together the three elements of God which we celebrate during the Church year. God is with us yet beyond us: God the creator; God made human in Jesus; God the Holy Spirit. God is three persons, yet one.

Where are the stories?

Bible stories

- Matthew 3.13-17 (Jesus' baptism)
- John 14.8-17 (Jesus speaks of another helper)
- 2 Corinthians 13.13 (The Grace)

Other sources

- The historic creeds of the Church
- St Patrick's Breastplate
- Many Celtic prayers
- The story of St Patrick and the shamrock: Once, Patrick was asked, 'How can there be only one God when you talk about God the Father, God the Son and God the Holy Spirit? That sounds like three Gods!' Patrick pointed to the three-lobed leaf of a shamrock. 'Look at the leaf. It has three parts yet it is only one leaf. In the same way God has three forms, yet is one God.'

What can we do to celebrate?

Make

A Trinity triangle

Copy the pattern below onto paper or card.

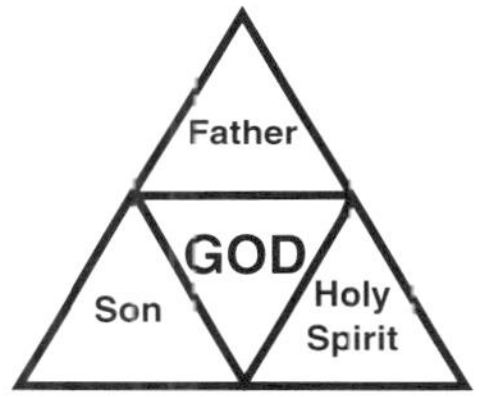

Careful measuring is needed! Use compasses and a protractor or set square.

Illustrate each section with pictures or decorations showing ways in which we see God:

- **Father – Creator**. God made the world, so show the world of Creation.
- **The Son** – Jesus the **pattern.** Jesus came to live on earth as a human to show us how God wants us to live. So show some events from his life or some of his teachings.
- **The Holy Spirit** – God living in **people** today. The Holy Spirit helps us to do God's will in the world. Draw or stick on pictures of people who are working for God in different ways.

Shamrock biscuits

Use your favourite basic biscuit recipe. Use a 'club'-shaped cutter or shape the biscuits by hand. If appropriate, cover them with green icing once they have cooled. Put them in packs of three to give away.

A kaleidoscope

You will need: a 15cm square of mirror board (available in craft shops); plain paper; tracing paper; felt-tipped pens; a pencil; tape; scissors; a ruler.

Using the pencil and ruler, divide the plain side of the mirror board into three sections, each 5cm wide.

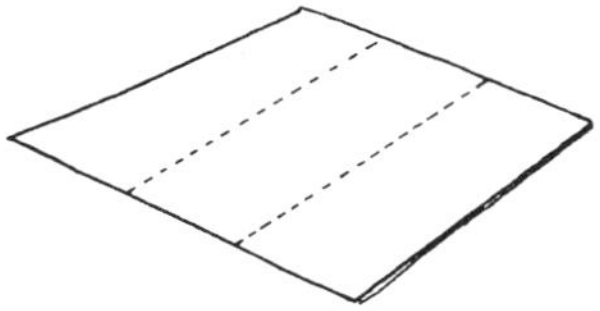

Score along the lines using the ruler and the tip of the scissors, taking care not to cut right through the card.

Fold the mirror board along the scored lines, so that the mirror is inside. Stick the edges together with tape.

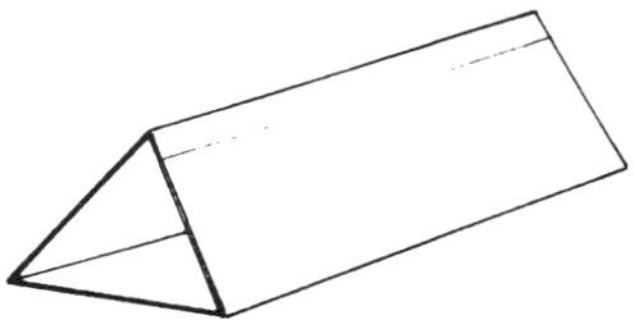

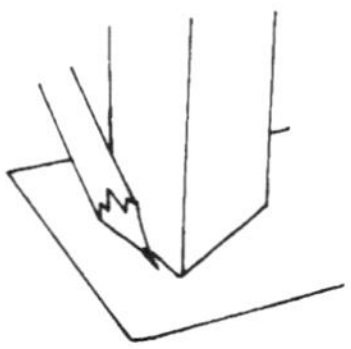

Stand the tube on the tracing paper and draw round the end. Do the same on the plain paper, and cut out the two triangles of paper.

Stick the triangle of tracing paper over one end of the tube. Colour some scraps of tracing paper with the pens. Cut the scraps into small pieces and put them inside the tube.

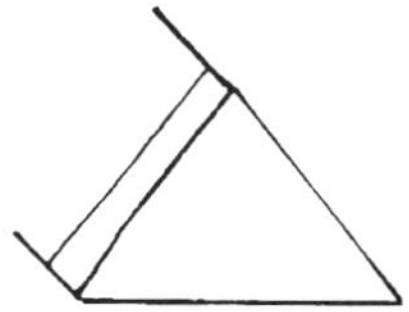

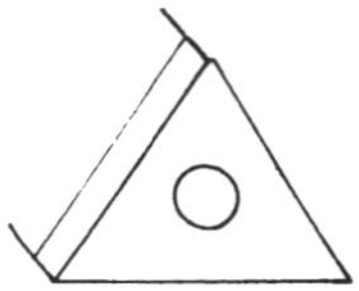

Cover the other end of the tube with the plain paper triangle. Use a pencil to punch a hole in the centre.

Hold the tube up to the light, and look through the hole to see the patterns change.

A Trinity upside-down pudding

Place three pineapple rings in the base of a baking tin before pouring sponge mixture on top.

A Trinity spinning top

Use a pair of compasses to cut a 5cm circle of card. Divide the circle into three equal segments, each of 120 degrees. Colour each segment differently. Put a sharpened matchstick through the central point. Spin until the three colours look like one.

Shamrock prints

Cut a round potato in half. Dip the cut face of the potato into thick paint. Print three potato shapes to make a shamrock leaf design.

Do

Water

Explore how water (H_2O) changes from ice, to water, to water vapour (steam is condensing water vapour) – three states, one substance.

Clover leaves

Find some well-shaped clover leaves and put them in a small vase.

Sing

'Father, we adore you'

Peruvian Gloria (See page 76)

What does it all add up to?

Questions

How does the idea of the Trinity help your idea of God?

In which aspect(s) of the Trinity do you see God let loose in the world? How?

Insight

God is greater than anything we can grasp, and yet, if we are willing, he makes himself known to us.

Actions

Find ways to give, share and receive. You may be able to do it all in one go, e.g. using a box of chocolates.

Prayer and Reflection

Ask three members of the family to bring to the table three symbols and to speak about each. Here are some suggestions in case you get stuck:

- a flower or large leaf symbolizing God the creator;
- a cross made from two twigs symbolizing Jesus;
- a lighted candle symbolizing God the Spirit.

Do you want to know what goes on at the heart of the Trinity? I'll tell you.
At the heart of the Trinity
the Father laughs, and gives birth to the Son.
The Son then laughs back at the Father,
and gives birth to the Spirit.
Then the whole Trinity laughs,
and gives birth to us.
(Meister Eckhart (1260-1327))

THANKING GOD (Harvest and Hallowtide)

Colour – green

What are we celebrating?

The fruitfulness of autumn leads into the dormancy and regeneration of the earth, with its cold, darkness and mystery.

A time for:

- giving thanks for ripe grains, fruit and vegetables;
- being conscious of the changes of the seasons as we move from autumn into winter;
- growing more aware of God as creator;
- confronting evil and acknowledging our fears;
- recognizing the cycle of life, death and new life;
- remembering and honouring those who have died.

Autumn is both the time of fruitfulness and the time when nature seems to stop, to come to an end. The shortening of the days, the falling of the leaves, the chill in the air, all point us to the rhythm of nature. As the trees shed their leaves, not only in preparation for the rigours of winter but also to dispose of rubbish, so, traditionally, people have faced winter by confronting the rubbish – the evil – in their own experience. **Hallowe'en** was traditionally the opportunity to confront all that is unholy in order to make a fresh start.

The earth appears to die, but in fact becomes dormant. We remember those who have died but live on as part of the 'communion of saints', particularly remembered on **All Saints**' and **All Souls**' Days.

The dead leaves and compost of autumn give to the sleeping earth the power to re-awaken. So the experiences of **All Hallows Tide** prepare us for Incarnation, new life in Christ.

What are the traditions?

❊ **Harvest:**

- a corn dolly was made from the last sheaf of the harvest to symbolize what was needed for new growth;
- a harvest supper was held to celebrate the completion of the harvest;
- harvest loaves were made with the first milling of the corn.

❊ **Hallowe'en**:

- based on the ancient Celtic fire festival, which marked the death of old life to make way for the new;
- fires were lit to burn up the rubbish in the fields;
- people believed that the dead returned to their old homes to be warmed and fed;
- witches and demons were placated with food;

- in the Middle Ages, Hallowe'en became part of the Christian festival of All Hallows/All Saints/All Souls.

❊ **All Saints:**
- from AD 605 the day was celebrated to remember all those saints who were not important enough to have their own day!

❊ **All Souls:**
- all the dead, known and unknown, were remembered – the communion of saints;
- 'soul cakes' were left out for the souls of those who had died. They were given to the poor and to children.

What stories lead us in?

❊ **Harvest:**
Deuteronomy 26.1-11
(The festival of first fruits)

❊ **Hallowe'en:**
Genesis 3.1-15
(The loss of human innocence)

❊ **All Saints:**
Revelation 7.9-12
(John's vision of the whole people of God)

❊ **All Souls:**
1 Thessalonians 4.13-14
(The hope of resurrection through Jesus)

What can we do to prepare?

❊ Observe the **changes in nature**, including the shortening days.

❊ Set up a **display corner**. This could include dried leaves and berries, corn and autumn fruits.

❊ Collect material, e.g. garden rubbish, for a **bonfire**.

❊ Think of how to mark this time of year in ways which celebrate our **Christian understanding**, growing beyond our 'pagan' origins.

Prayer and Reflection

What a rich harvest your goodness provides!
Wherever you go there is plenty.
The pastures are filled with flocks;
the hillsides are full of joy.
The fields are covered with sheep;
the valleys are full of wheat.
Everything shouts and sings for joy.
(Psalm 65.11-13)

A grain of wheat remains no more than a single grain unless it is dropped into the ground and dies. If it does die, then it produces many grains.
(John 12.24)

Harvest Thanksgiving

What are we celebrating?

We recognize God's generosity in the fact that the earth has once again produced food.

Where are the stories?

Bible stories

- Genesis 8.22
  (Seedtime and harvest will not fail)
- Genesis 41.1-8, 25-36
  (Pharaoh's dream)
- Mark 4.26-29
  (The seed growing secretly)

Other stories

- *The Enormous Turnip*
  (Traditional)
- *The Giant Jam Sandwich*
  Lord and Burroway (Pan)
- *Lark Rise to Candleford*
  Flora Thompson (OUP)
- Also stories from the developing world through Christian Aid and other materials

What can we do to celebrate?

Make

A corn dolly

Use straw to make a corn dolly.

Bread

Bake a harvest loaf, plait or wheatsheaf with mice.

A harvest basket

You will need: a margarine tub; coloured paper or wrapping paper; a strip of card; a stapler, glue or tape.

Cover the margarine tub with the paper. Attach the card with staples, tape or glue to make a handle. Fill the basket with flowers or cakes or both.

A harvest collage

Make a harvest collage using pasta, lentils, corn, seed heads, autumn leaves, conkers, nuts etc. Write the words 'Praise the Lord of the harvest' in the centre.

Find out

Where does our food come from and who grows it? Is it fairly traded?

Eat

Make a special harvest meal. Invite someone to share it.
Grow some of your own food (e.g.cress or bean sprouts) and eat it together..
Pick blackberries and use them to make a crumble, pie or jam.

Play

Go through the alphabet and see how many things you can think of to thank God for.

Sing

'When God made the garden of creation' (*Come and Praise*)

'We plough the fields and scatter'

'First the seed and then the rain' (*Big Blue Planet*)

Look

Colours

Notice harvest colours: the red, orange and purple of berries, the changing colours of leaves etc.

The harvest

If possible, watch harvesting in progress.

Smell

Enjoy the scents of autumn: fallen leaves, bonfires, baking bread, ripe apples, freshly-picked tomatoes.

Listen

Notice the wind blowing through the corn or the dead leaves.

What does it all add up to?

Questions

Why does a good God allow some people to have plenty while others starve or live at subsistence level?

Do you agree with the view that the world's problems are so big that we haven't a hope of changing them?

Insight

If we were to share across the world, no one would need to go hungry. God is generous; we are selfish.

Actions

Say grace regularly, encouraging all the family to sit down together for meals:

For every cup and plateful,
Lord, make us truly grateful.

Prayer and Reflection

The silver rain, the shining sun,
The fields where scarlet poppies run
And all the ripples of the wheat
Are in the bread that I do eat.
So when I sit for every meal
And say a grace I always feel
That I am eating rain and sun
And fields where scarlet poppies run.
(Alice C Henderson)

All-Hallows Eve (Hallowe'en)

What are we celebrating?

On All-Hallows Eve we both face the reality of evil and defy it in order to make a fresh start. In recent years Hallowe'en has become a very popular festival with children, giving them the opportunity to dress up as witches and ghosts and celebrate the American custom of 'Trick or Treat'. Some aspects of these practices have led to very great concern and calls for new ways of celebrating the festival.

Where are the stories?

Bible stories

- Genesis 3.1-15
  (Adam and Eve's disobedience)
- Genesis 4.1-16
  (Cain murders Abel)
- Daniel 6
  (Daniel in the lions' den)
- Romans 5.12-19
  (Adam and Christ)

Other stories

- *The Last Battle*
  CS Lewis (Collins/Lions)
- *Fungus the Bogeyman*
  Raymond Briggs (Hamish Hamilton)
- *The Twits*
  Roald Dahl (Puffin)
- *Where the wild things are*
  Maurice Sendak (Puffin)
- *A lion in the meadow*
  Margaret Mahy (Puffin)
- Also many fairy stories, e.g. *Hansel and Gretel*

What can we do to celebrate?

Make

Soul cakes

These were traditionally made on All Souls' Day:

Soul cakes:

450g plain white flour
60g soft margarine
60g granulated sugar
1 egg
Sachet easy-blend yeast
1½ tblsp milk
1 tsp allspice

Grease a baking tray. Rub the margarine into the flour. Add the other ingredients. Work into a light dough. Cover and put in a warm place for about 30 minutes to rise. Divide into small pieces and place on baking tray. Cover and allow to rise for 15 minutes. Cook for 15 minutes at gas mark 7 or 220° C.

A pumpkin lantern

Hollow out a pumpkin to make a lantern. Cut windows in the shell. Place a nightlight or candle inside it. Roast the seeds and eat them with salt. Make pumpkin pie with the flesh you have hollowed out.

Pumpkin pie:

225g pastry
2 beaten eggs
110g sugar
225-350g cooked pumpkin flesh
pinch grated nutmeg
2 tsp cinnamon
½tsp salt
140 ml milk
whipped cream

Line a flan dish with pastry. Mix together the ingredients for the filling. Put into the pastry case. Bake at gas mark 6 or 200° C for about 40 minutes until the pastry is brown and the filling set. Serve topped with whipped cream.

A bonfire

Light a bonfire to get rid of all the rubbish which has accumulated during the summer. Wrap large potatoes in foil and cook them in the bonfire. Fill them with butter or cheese and eat them in the open air. You could also bake chestnuts in the fire. (Don't forget to pierce them first.)

Visit

As a family (do not encourage children to go on their own) take soul cakes as gifts to friends and neighbours. Ask them to say the old North Country refrain before you hand over the cakes: 'A soul cake, a soul cake, I pray thee good mistress, a soul cake'.

Talk

If possible, make the opportunity to talk about things of which children are frightened (not just ghosts and witches). 'The dark' may come near the top of the list.

Think about bad things which are going on in the world. Decide on something constructive which can be done, perhaps giving a gift to a mutually-agreed charity or other, more specific, action.

Play

Apple-bobbing

This is a traditional game. Fill a bucket or basin with water and put it on the floor. It is a good idea to cover the area with a groundsheet or plastic tablecloth. Float apples in the water. In turn, kneel down with your hands behind your back and try to grab an apple with your teeth. Have plenty of towels on hand!

Variations: if any members of the group have difficulty in kneeling on the floor, put the bucket or basin on a table and provide a chair for participants to sit or kneel on as required. Nuts in their shells can also be floated in the water, but be sure that no one is allergic to nuts.

Sing

'Kindle a flame to lighten the dark'. (See page 77)

What does it all add up to?

Questions

Why have people celebrated Hallowe'en for centuries?

How do we feel as autumn turns into winter?

Why is this time often associated with evil?

What good news is there for Christians at this time of the year?

Insights

'Goodness is stronger than evil;
Love is stronger than hate;
Light is stronger than darkness;
Life is stronger than death;
Victory is ours through Him who loves us.'
Desmond Tutu

Actions

Consider what things frighten you and those who are close to you. Decide what action to take to help to destroy these fears.

Prayer and Reflection

From ghoulies and ghosties,
Long leggety beasties
And things that go bump in the night
Good Lord, deliver us.
(Traditional Cornish)

Sometimes, when Celtic saints were troubled by evil or attacked by enemies, they made a circle round themselves, calling for the presence of God to protect them.

Christ be with me, Christ within me,
Christ behind me, Christ before me,
Christ beside me, Christ to win me,
Christ to comfort and restore me,
Christ beneath me, Christ above me,
Christ in quiet, Christ in danger,
Christ in hearts of all that love me,
Christ in mouth of friend and stranger.
(St Patrick's Breastplate, versified by Cecil Frances Alexander)

Dear God,
Help me to know what's good or bad.
It isn't easy you know.
(Anon)

All Saints (All-Hallows) and All Souls

What are we celebrating?

On All Saints' Day we remember people who have died who were important to the Church. On All Souls' Day we remember people who have died who have been important in our own lives.

Where are the stories?

Bible stories

- Romans 1.7
  (Greetings to the saints) – GNB translates the Greek word which means saints as 'his own people'
- Ephesians 2.19
  (We are all called to be saints) – GNB translates the Greek word which means saints as 'God's people'

Other stories

- *Saints for all Seasons*
  Victor J Green
- *Five minutes a saint*
  John Foster (Epworth)
- *The Diary of Anne Frank*
- *Pray with....*
  Brother Kenneth and Sister Geraldine (CHP/NS)

What can we do to celebrate?

Make

A chain of saints

Cut out a chain of saints, as for the prophet lantern (see page 12). Will you choose famous saints, or present-day 'saints' whom you know personally, or a mixture? Glue your saints round a jam jar with a small nightlight in it. Use it as a table decoration and also as a focus for prayer.

A saint symbol

Draw three circles on a triangle of paper to make the Irish symbol for a saint. Pray for a 'saint' you know.

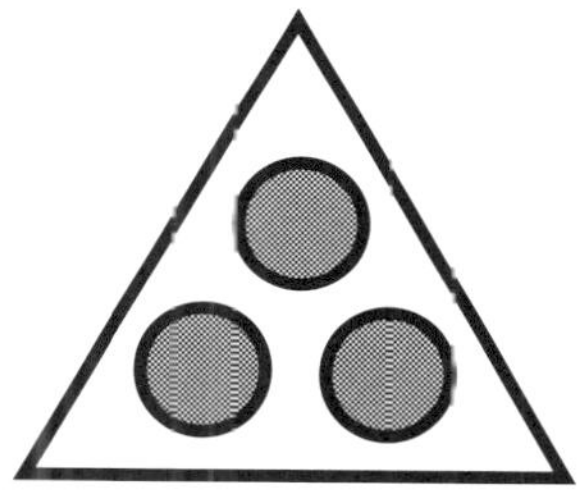

Do

Pumpkin lantern

Relight your Hallowe'en lantern and name someone you consider a saint as you do so.

Pray together

Think of one good or saintly thing about each member of your family. Share your ideas then light a candle or say a prayer of thanksgiving for one another.

Family memories

Look at family photograph albums. Recall stories and events involving your family, alive and dead. Try to remember fun times you have had together as well as solemn occasions.

Family tree

Make a family tree. Make sure you are all in it.

Visit

Go to a local church which is named after a saint, perhaps one you do not normally attend. Find out all you can about the saint after whom the church is named. Look for reminders of the saint in the church, such as stained glass windows or carvings.

Eat

Share soul cakes (see the recipe on page 70).

Find out

Discover as much as possible about a more modern saint such as Martin Luther King, Mother Teresa, Oscar Romero or someone who is loved and respected in your home church or town. Put together a poster or scrapbook about them.

Sing

'Sing praise to God whose light on Julian shined' (*Story Song*)

'For all the saints'

'When the saints go marching in'

Write

Make up your own obituary or epitaph.

Talk

Talk about death, and the experience of losing a loved one.

Talk about fear of the unknown.

Talk about your glimpses of heaven through great experiences.

What does it all add up to?

? **Questions**

Why do we need to celebrate the lives of saints?

What makes a person a saint?

Why do we admire them?

In what ways should we try to copy them?

What do you think their brothers and sisters think/thought of them?

Do you have to be a Christian to be a saint?

☆ **Insights**

Saints are people who try hard to do what God wants them to do. Most of them are not extra-special people in the eyes of others, but to God they are very special people.

We are all called to be saints.

➜ **Actions**

'For the saints of God are just like me
And I mean to be one too!'

Try to put this into practice.

Prayer and Reflection

I sing a song of the saints of God,
Patient and brave and true,
Who toiled and fought and lived and died
For the Lord they loved and knew.
And one was a doctor, and one was a queen,
And one was a shepherdess on the green:
They were all of them saints of God; and I mean,
God helping, to be one too.

They loved their Lord so good and dear,
And his love made them strong;
And they followed the right, for Jesus' sake,
The whole of their good lives long.
And one was a soldier, and one was a priest,
And one was slain by a fierce wild beast:
And there's not any reason, no, not the least,
Why I shouldn't be one too.

They lived not only in ages past, there are hundreds of thousands still;
The world is bright with the joyous saints
Who loved to do Jesus' will.
You can meet them in school, or in lanes, or at sea,
In church, or in trains, or in shops, or at tea,
For the saints of God are just like me,
And I mean to be one too.
(Lesbia Scott and others)

Saints are stained-glass bright,
letting the God-light shine through.
So many colours!
(Author unknown)

Glory to God

Source unknown, probably Peruvian

1. **Leader** Glory to God, Glory to God
Glory to the Father.
Everyone Glory to God, Glory to God
Glory to the Father.
Leader To God be glory for ever.
Everyone To God be glory for ever.
Leader Alleluia, Amen.
Everyone Alleluia, Amen.
Divide in 2 Alleluia, Amen.
Divide in 3 Alleluia, Amen.

2. **Leader** Glory to God, Glory to God
Glory to Christ Jesus.
Everyone Glory to God, Glory to God
Glory to Christ Jesus.
Leader To God be glory for ever.
Everyone To God be glory for ever.
Leader Alleluia, Amen.
Everyone Alleluia…

3. **Leader** Glory to God, Glory to God
Glory to the Spirit
Everyone Glory to God, Glory to God
Glory to the Spirit
Leader To God be glory for ever.
Everyone To God be glory for ever.
Leader Alleluia, Amen.
Everyone Alleluia…

Kindle a Flame to Lighten the Dark

The Iona Community

Acknowledgements

The editors and publishers gratefully acknowledge permission to reproduce the following material but, if any rights have inadvertently been overlooked, the necessary correction will gladly be made in subsequent editions.

Page 8: 'When Noah's Ark was high and dry' by Fred Kaan, from *Pilgrim Praise,* Galliard, 1968. Used by permission.

Page 11: a verse of 'The world was in darkness' from *Let God's Children sing*, Geoffrey Chapman. Permission sought.

Page 11: 'I saw a stable' from 'The Safety of the World' from *The Christmas Road*, Church House Publishing 1986, © The Central Board of Finance of the Church of England. Used by permission.

Page 17: a prayer by a New Guinea Christian, from *Essential Book of Christmas,* Lion. Permission sought.

Page 20: 'Not for him' by Daniel Salsedo, from *Festivals Pack,* Philip Green. Permission sought.

Page 23: 'It looks...' by Ann Lewin, from *Candles and Kingfishers.* Permission sought.

Page 23: an extract from 'Journey of the Magi' by TS Eliot. Permission sought.

Page 27: 'Green-hearted snowdrop' by Kate McIlhagga, from *Encompassing Presence*, the URC 1995 Prayer Handbook. Used by permission of Kate McIlhagga.

Page 27: 'Lent is a time for new beginnings', from *Rejoice 2*, HarperCollins Religious. Permission sought.

Page 30: a version of Psalm 150 by Jan Pickard, from *Connect* magazine. Used by permission of Jan Pickard.

Page 32: 'Ashing' by Ann Lewin, from *By the Way*. Permission sought.

Page 35: 'Loving God...' by Paul Leingang, from *Partners in Learning,* 1995. Used by permission.

Page 35: a verse of 'God, you hold me, like a mother' by Andrew Pratt, from *Big Blue Planet*, Stainer & Bell, 1995. Used by permission.

Page 37: the Redemption Calendar, from *Christmas & Easter Ideas Book* by Oliver and Ianthe Pratt, Steed & Ward. Used by permission.

Page 38: 'The Donkey's Owner' by Clive Sansom from *The Witness*, David Higham Associates. Used by permission.

Page 38: a verse of 'Christ is coming' by Cynthia Dean and Lothian Road Church Primary School, from *Big Blue Planet*, Stainer & Bell, 1995. Permission sought.

Page 40: 'A carol for Holy Week' by Pamela Egan, from *Words for Easter*, National Society/Church House Publishing 1990, © The National Society (Church of England) for Promoting of Religious Education. Used by permission.

Page 41: Jerusalem City Map from *Partners in Learning,* 1988. Used by permission.

Page 43: 'Three Tables' by Donald Hilton from *Flowing Streams,* edited by Donald Hilton, NCEC, 1993. Used by permission of Donald Hilton.

Page 46: 'There is a man...' by Amy, aged 10, from *Christianity Topic Book 3* by Margaret Cooling. Permission sought.

Page 47: 'The Bamboo Tree' from *Alive in God's World*, Church Information Office 1968, © the Wadderton Group. Used by permission.

Page 50: 'Waiting' by an anonymous 14-year-old, from *Flowing Streams*, edited by Donald Hilton, NCEC.

Page 50: a verse of 'When I'mfeeling down and sad' by Joy Webb, from *Big Blue Planet*, Stainer & Bell, 1995. Used by permission.

Page 51: 'The Enterprising Grub' from *Alive in God's World,* Church Information Office 1968, © the Wadderton Group. Used by permission.

Page 54: 'How can he tell...' by A Elliott Cameron, from *Festivals Pack,* Philip Green. Permission sought.

Page 56: 'God has put a circle round us' by Jenny Dann, from *Big Blue Planet*, Stainer & Bell, 1995. Permission sought.

Page 57: a verse of 'Jesus' love is very wonderful' by HW Rattle. Used by permission of Scripture Union.

Page 58: 'I wonder how you would do it nowadays?' from *Live and Pray*, Church Information Office 1970, © the Community of the Glorious Ascension Deaconess Community of St Andrew. Used by permission.

Page 61: two verses of 'Morning, evening, frost and dew' by Doreen Newport, from *Big Blue Planet*, Stainer & Bell. Permission sought.

Page 61: Three verses of 'God as fire, send your Spirit now' by Judy Jarvis, from *Story Song*, Stainer & Bell. Permission sought.

Page 69: 'The silver rain, the shining sun' by Alice C Henderson, from *Festivals Pack*, Philip Green. Permission sought.

Page 72: 'Goodness is stronger than evil...' by Desmond Tutu, from *An African Prayer Book*, ed. Desmond Tutu, Hodder & Stoughton. Permission sought.

Page 75: ' I sing a song of the saints of God' by Lesbia Scott and others, from *BBC Hymn Book*, Oxford University Press. Permission sought.

Page 75: 'Saints are stained-glass bright', from *Rejoice 2*, HarperCollins Religious. Permission sought.

Page 77: 'Kindle a flame to lighten the dark' by the Iona Community, from *Wild Goose Songs 1*. Permission sought.

All Bible quotations are taken from the Good News Bible second edition, © 1994, unless otherwise indicated.